Contents

Contents   vii

Preface to the First Edition

Health economics is still a relatively young science. It is only in the past decade or so that economists in the United Kingdom have begun in earnest to consider how the discipline of economics can be used to assist planning and decision-making in health care. At the present time there is no book available which combines some simple, easily understood economic techniques with a full awareness of the problems of decision-making in health care and with guidelines as to how the approach of health economics can be introduced and used at different levels of health care management and planning. This book is intended to fill this gap and is based on the practical experiences over the past five years of a small team of economists and health care staff who have introduced such principles and techniques to their colleagues and into the day-to-day working of a health board.

The philosophy of economics is perhaps just as important, if not more so, than the application of economic techniques. Economics does not seek to alter the values of different groups but it does try to understand them and set them in a framework of choice so that the implications of the different choices are clearly identified. Such valuation is central to planning and decision-making in health care but all too seldom are the values made explicit. These are the prime issues to which economics can be applied in health care although there is still much to be done at the practical level to improve the relevant concepts, theories and techniques. This book attempts to show how best to apply the approaches in health care planning and how it might be achieved.

It is inevitable that in advocating greater rationality and explicitness in health care planning and decision-making criticisms are made of the health service. Such criticisms, however, are intended to be constructive. For those interested in how the health service

functions and how it might be made to function better, it is hoped
that this book will provide some relevant food for thought.

Department of Community Medicine   G. H. M.
University of Aberdeen   E. M. R.
January 1979   R. D. W.

Preface to the Second Edition

More than six years on from writing the preface to the first edition of this text, we find that little has changed. That comment may seem somewhat odd to those in the health service who suffered yet another reorganisation in 1982 and who are currently unsettled by the changes going through as a result of the Griffiths initiative. None the less there are perhaps greater grounds for optimism than six years ago; the attempts to introduce budgeting changes and to provide management information are examples of new opportunities. But these will be of little benefit without a willingness to understand and use the information that is becoming available.

In the second edition we have updated where necessary the material we used previously to exemplify the contribution the techniques of economic analysis can make to such understanding and use. We have also attempted to reflect the management changes that have occurred without trying to forecast where those are likely to lead the service. Wherever that might be economics has an important part to play. In that respect nothing has changed.

Department of Community Medicine
University of Aberdeen
June 1985

G. H. M.
E. M. R.
R. D. W.

Acknowledgements

Many people have contributed in several ways to the writing of this book, to discussions surrounding many of the ideas expressed and to some of the studies reported. We are indebted, in no small measure, to Ianthe Dingwall Fordyce for her penetrating but always constructive criticism and statistical assistance. Our particular thanks are also due to the members of the Health Economics Research Unit and the Department of Political Economy, both of Aberdeen University, and to numerous officers of Grampian Health Board. We are grateful to Isabel Tudhope for the repeated drafts she prepared and to the Scottish Home and Health Department for financial support for some of the research outlined in the book.

Any remaining errors and the opinions expressed are, of course, the responsibility of the authors alone.

1
Choices for Health Care

The need for choice

From the standpoint of social security, a health service providing full preventive and creative treatment of every kind to every
citizen without exceptions, without remuneration limit and
without an economic barrier at any point to delay recourse to it,
is the ideal plan ... The primary interest of the Ministry of
Social Security is not in the details of the national health service
or in its financial arrangements. It is in finding a health service
which will diminish disease by prevention and cure [1].

Before the National Health Service was created, choices for health
care were clearly recognised by the public, most of whom had to
judge for themselves the occasions on which they could afford to
seek medical care – as well as those on which they could not
'afford' to do without. When the health service was established,
the need for choices did not disappear but it did become obscured
by a number of factors. The philosophy expressed at that time was
that the health service should and would provide the *best* possible
medical care for *everyone*. The stock of ill health would gradually
be eroded by the quality and comprehensiveness of the services so
that, ultimately, the health of the population would increase, the
demands made on the service would diminish and the proportion
of the gross national product devoted to health care would fall[36].
In effect, the aim was to remove the need for individuals to make
choices about how much of which health care to have because
there would be sufficient care to cope with all ill health. The one
issue of choice which was acknowledged to remain was the speed
at which the service could accomplish its aims; this choice rested
with the government who would decide how much money to

1

devote annually to health care. The fact that short-term choices of what to buy first with the money would have to be made at each successive level of the emerging structure, from the departments of health to the professionals within the caring services, was brushed aside by the enthusiasm of the desire for the long-term ideal. Indeed, some would say that central government control was intended to be sufficiently tight that most of these short-term choices would be pre-empted and only the medical profession would be left with any choice of priorities about who should receive what type of care.

It is now history that events did not follow this course. Yet, despite clear evidence that the service would – and did – grow at a relatively rapid pace through both the 1950s and 1960s, the initial expectation of providing the best at falling cost resulted in an unfortunate legacy, the apparent lack of willingness to accept that choices not only had to be made but were being made, and the continuation of the view that the place to be was always on the technological frontier of medicine because this was the 'best' medical care meant the breeding of a reluctance to make rational choices in the allocation of health care resources. This, more than anything else, is responsible for many of the management problems and other difficulties which are now built in to the health service.

The need for choice in the allocation of resources in health care arises directly because the resources available are limited, and the demands made on these resources appear at times almost insatiable. From this arises the idea of 'opportunity cost'. This simple but important concept acknowledges that in allocating scarce resources to a particular service a sacrifice is made in that an opportunity of obtaining some other benefit is forgone. Despite some attempts to cling to the belief that all would be well if only more resources were made available to the health service, there has been an increasing awareness within the service in the past few years that choices have to be made and sometimes rather brutally. Along with awareness, there has been a growing search for tools with which to formulate more rational approaches to planning and management in health care. In addition, the issues of choice and priorities within health care have entered public debate via several recent central government white papers and related documents which contain specific proposals about the nature of priorities and ways in which resources might correspondingly be reallocated [15, 16, 17, 59, 62].

Since its inception, the NHS has witnessed a number of reorganisations, most recently in the move away from the concept of consensus management with the appointment of General Managers, as recommended in the Griffiths Report [20]. In some ways this change is to be welcomed in the context of gaining greater acceptance and use of economics in health care since it is part of an acknowledgement that increased rational management of the health service is desirable.

Why economics?

Economics has been defined as 'the study of how men and society end up choosing, with or without the use of money, to employ scarce productive resources that could have alternative uses, to produce various commodities and distribute them for consumption, now or in the future, among various people and groups in society. It analyses the costs and benefits of improving patterns of resource allocation' [55].

The central issues which the authors believe confront the policy-makers and decision-makers in the health service in the 1980s are:

(1) the need to determine what services to provide, when and at what level of provision;
(2) the need to determine how and where to provide such services;
(3) the need to determine who should get the services.

If these are the main issues, then it is logical to turn to that discipline whose philosophy is specifically aimed at overcoming some of the problems associated with these issues.

The application of economic techniques and the philosophy of economics has been growing, albeit slowly, in health care. While North America has seen a now lengthening history and an explosion of interest in health economics, in the United Kingdom the science of health economics has only just reached its late teens. In 1967 Feldstein's [28] study of the British National Health

Service represented a milestone as the beginning of a decade of increasing interest not only of economists in health care but also of health-care personnel in economics. However, it is only in the past ten years that health economics has become established as a field in its own right. As a result there is still a comparatively small British literature in health economics, although that part of health economics which is directly concerned with assisting in health services decision-making and planning has perhaps been growing most rapidly. (See, for example, Drummond and Mooney [26], Lee and Mills [41].)

One of the major difficulties with health service planning and hence the application of economics to health care problems in the United Kingdom is that the National Health Service does not operate in the same way as a private firm. In the private sector prices exist for goods and services; in the health service the great majority of services are 'zero-priced' at the point of consumption. This creates a number of problems. (These are not unique to public health care systems. For example, under many health insurance schemes prices are zero at the point of consumption).

In private markets consumers use prices as signals or indicators of how much income they have to forgo to obtain a particular good or service. In deciding whether to purchase goods and services and how much to purchase of which, consumers consider the satisfaction they expect to obtain from the wide range available. The greater the satisfaction the consumer expects to obtain from a particular good, the higher the value he will attach to it and hence the higher the price the consumer will be prepared to pay for it.

Prices are therefore important as signals to consumers and as such are important indicators to the economist of consumers' preferences. Without prices – as in the case of health care – certain difficulties arise, particularly on the question of how to value services of health care and indeed whose values it is appropriate to use. The issue of valuation is thus one of major importance in this book.

A common assumption in economics is that the best judge of a consumer's own preferences is the consumer and consequently it is the consumer's own values which should be used to place values on the goods and services which he chooses to consume. This of course assumes that the individual consumer has the capacity, knowledge and desire to make the necessary value judgements.

But this is only one, if a fairly common, judgement surrounding the question of valuation in economics. It can also be argued that in some instances individual consumers are not the best judge of the valuation of goods and services and that consequently some agent (the State for example) may act on the consumer's behalf. This paternalistic approach is perhaps best exemplified in the compulsory education of children.

In health care, *que faire?* There is a considerable and growing debate about this question of valuation in health care but it can for the present be circumvented in a practical way. Since we do not at the current time know what values consumers (patients and potential patients) place on the outputs of health care we cannot use consumers' values. This does not mean that the consumers' preferences should be totally ignored. (For example, if a breast cancer screening service were to be established the likely utilisation of the service, which would to some extent reflect consumers' values and preferences, would need to be taken into account.) What it does mean is that for the present and the immediate future the value judgements and the values used in health care will largely remain the prerogative of the government, the medical profession and the existing institutional decision-makers. Accepting the existing valuation processes does not, however, imply that they are ideal; only that there is in the immediate future no alternative. Again it does not mean that consumers' preferences are ignored but, rather that the judgement of the existing decision-makers has to be accepted as to how far the values they adopt should attempt to reflect those of consumers.

For producers in a private market, prices are again important signals. They indicate to producers the revenue they can obtain from the sale of their goods. They thus represent important influences on how much the producer can afford to spend to produce goods and still make a profit. The important consideration here is that the producer in deciding on which goods to produce, how many, of what quality and what production processes to use, is much affected by the prices he is likely to obtain for his products. When, as in health care, services are 'sold' at zero-price some of the effects are missing or at least muted. This makes the problem of trying to make the best use of available resources more difficult, but the techniques of economics can assist in deciding how best to determine relative priorities and allocate resources to different policies.

The signals which prices represent can also act as incentives and disincentives. Thus the removal of prices at the point of consumption with the formation of the NHS reduced the cost to the consumer of using health care. Indeed it was part of the rationale for the health service to increase equity by removing price barriers. Yet by doing so and placing the great majority of health care professionals on a salaried or per capitation remuneration system an important incentive mechanism was removed from the supply side. Indeed it is one of the failings of the NHS that it is only recently that it has been acknowledged that incentives on the supply side need to be strengthened. This has led, *inter alia*, to important discussions both in the Griffiths Report [20] and in research circles more generally [69] about the need for changes in the budgeting structure, in particular for the implementation of budgets for clinical teams.

Given that the resources available to the health services are limited, the issues of choice in the health service are very real. It is simply not possible to have an objective of providing 'the best health care for all'. This is not a function of the current economic climate, although this has perhaps done much to make policy-makers aware of the realities of choice; it would still be the case if the health service budget were larger.

The aim of providing 'the best' within the constraint of available resources is, however, an objective to which the health service ought to ascribe – but this is a very different definition of 'best'. Such a definition accepts that resources are scarce and accepts that the concept of opportunity cost is central to policy-making. At the same time it is a more difficult objective with which to work. Indeed we may well want to temper this efficiency objective with some concern for equity.

Once the concept of opportunity cost is accepted there is nothing which is 'absolute'; all values are relative. Different objectives require differential relative values. Relative weights have to be attached to different outputs. It is not just a question of defining waste in terms of inefficiency or using resources uneconomically when the same output could be achieved more cheaply. If resources are used ineffectively, in the sense of using them to produce a relatively low-valued output when a higher-valued output could be obtained, then there is also 'waste' in that less health or at least lower-valued health is being produced than is possible within the budgetary constraint.

Although much of this is perhaps accepted by health-care administrators, in practice the service has tended to operate under what may be described as 'disjointed incrementalism'. Decisions on resource allocation have tended to be taken in a narrow, 'one-off' framework. Too little attention has been given to the deployment of existing resources; even the discussion of how to deploy increments in resources has been conducted in a manner such that the broad issues of health-care objectives and priorities have been submerged in *ad hoc* low-level decisions.

There is no 'scientifically' right or wrong way of determining the allocation of resources to and within health care but there are ways which are likely to be better than others. Again the nature of health care is such that it is not possible to determine all decisions through some rational, synoptic planning approach. But the basic tenet of this book is that more rational, explicit health care planning is a good thing.

Value judgements are constantly being made within health care, although very often not explicitly; actual monetary values are, at least implicitly, being placed on different outputs. This follows from the fact that a decision to devote resources to, say, the setting up of a kidney unit implies that the benefits of so doing are at least equal to the costs of so doing. Conversely, a decision not to set up such a unit implies that the benefits are less than the costs. Thus to adopt the approaches and techniques of health economics and thereby a system of rational synoptic planning in which value judgements and values are made explicit will not involve any change of principle from what currently exists. Rather it will increase the awareness of policy-makers of the broad framework of objectives and relative priorities with which they are, perhaps unconsciously, already operating.

In essence therefore it is argued that within the health service there is scope for considerable improvement in decision-making and that the issues of what to provide, how and to whom, which are central to both the problems of the health service and the discipline of economics, can be helped by an injection of both the philosophy and the techniques of economics.

The problems of choice are real. Only if the concept of opportunity cost is both accepted and applied, can decision-making be made more rational and explicit thereby enabling the health service to improve its performance when facing such choices. The fact that choices are made by so many different groups at so many different levels about so many different matters makes the task a difficult one; but to assume that it is impossible is to close one's eyes to the prospect of improving health care planning, consequently, health care and, ultimately, health.

Outline

The book is essentially in four parts. The next three chapters explain certain approaches and techniques of economics which can assist in making choices for health. Chapters 5 to 7 present various case studies exemplifying the use of these approaches and techniques. Thereafter chapters 8 to 10 deal with the organisation of the National Health Service and some of the reasons why certain organisational changes could assist planning and give health economics more fertile soil in which to operate. Finally, chapter 11 suggests and discusses some of the choices that must be faced.

If choices for health care are to be made more rationally and explicitly then some kind of overview of the services being provided is desirable. Consequently chapter 2 introduces the reader to programme budgeting as a framework for planning. By providing cost data and related activity data in an appropriate form (for example by client groups such as the elderly) a framework can be presented for beginning to consider the relative priorities to be attached to the health care of such groups.

But choices have to be made both between these groups and within them. Chapter 3 introduces the concept of 'marginal analysis' as a framework for choosing between alternative patterns of care. Thereafter chapter 4 looks at the evaluation techniques of cost–benefit analysis and cost–effectiveness analysis which can assist the decision-maker in deciding whether or not to pursue a particular objective and if so how.

The approaches of programme budgeting, marginal analysis, cost–benefit and cost–effectiveness analysis are then given some flesh by presenting in chapters 5 to 7 some case studies exemplifying their use. Programme budgeting, as it has been applied within a Scottish health board, is outlined in chapter 5. The use of marginal analysis as an evaluative framework is shown in chapter 6, in this instance in the context of the balance of care of the elderly between the community, residential home and hospital. Thereafter chapter 7 highlights various aspects of cost–benefit and cost–effectiveness analyses from case studies on such subjects as provision of acute beds and screening for colonic cancer.

One of the difficulties in health-care planning is the diffuse decision-making structure of the service and the interactions which occur in the decision-making process between different levels and groups. Decisions are made and influenced by central government, regional authorities, health boards, districts, sectors and units; by consultative and advisory committees at national and local level; by individual clinicians; by local health councils and the public at large. This means that there is no single level or group at which the ideas of planning and hence of health economics should be aimed.

The nature of the choices to be made is also varied. Choices have to be made between hospital, community and primary care services; for particular client groups (for example the elderly); related to the different outputs of health care (for example chronic versus acute); on equity considerations; and about many other issues.

At all these levels and natures of choice and for all these different groups of decision-makers, different objectives may be relevant and different priorities and relative values may apply. Against this background a number of questions arise – Who should be concerned with which objectives? Who should make which decisions? How are the decision-makers to be orchestrated? Whose values are to be applied to which decisions? These questions are discussed in detail in chapters 8 to 10.

Finally, in chapter 11 the book concludes by indicating the need for more use of both the philosophy and techniques of economics in approaching the many problems currently faced by the health service and how this might be achieved. It is to be hoped that the reader who has made his way through the rest of the book will, by chapter 11, be more than ready to accept such conclusions and indeed the prospect of some further reorganisation of the health service to allow effective planning and a wider acceptance of the approaches of economics.

2
The Framework for Choice

In chapter 1 some of the problems associated with decision-making and planning in health-care have been mentioned. It is not suggested either that there is one single approach which can overcome all these problems or that there is a simple solution to them. None the less, in this and the next two chapters certain techniques are discussed which if applied can lead to improved decision-making in health care. This chapter deals with the framework for planning, the next two examine the framework and techniques for evaluation of options.

The first requirement for planning is to create an appropriate framework within which broad questions relating to health-care objectives, priorities and choices can be considered, that is, there is a need for an overview of the health-care system. Unless such an overview is created – and created in appropriate terms – there is a danger that planning in health care will continue to be obsessed with detail and the broad objectives and associated priorities of health care will not recieve the attention which they merit.

The approach of programme budgeting

The proposed framework for providing an overview for health care planning is based on programme budgeting. While the terms 'budgeting' and 'budgets' are normally applied to current and/or future allocations of expenditure, in the context of *programme* budgeting and *programme* budgets, it is assumed that they can be applied to past allocations as well.

There are several roles that programme budgeting can perform. In addition to its planning function it can also assist with control of expenditure as with any other form of budgeting. However, to be used in that way would require more detailed precise budgets than are required for planning purposes. Again it can assist in providing important incentive mechanisms for promoting efficiency such as is advocated for clinical budgeting (see Wickings *et al.*, [70]). Here it is the planning role that is of interest.

The principle underlying programme budgeting as a planning framework is very simple. If decisions are to be made about broadly defined health-care objectives and priorities – for example, what are the objectives associated with care of the elderly? What relative priorities are attached to the treatment of cancer compared with the prevention of heart disease? – then data should be provided in similarly broad terms to match the nature of the choices. Consequently it becomes desirable to provide information about the resources involved in for example all aspects of care of the elderly and to be able to relate this to the services being provided and the outputs achieved. This programme budgeting attempts to do.

But is the supposition correct? Does it matter if these broad objectives and priorities are not considered? Is it not possible – and indeed perhaps preferable – to ensure more simply that each and every decision is made in full awareness of the costs and benefits involved?

There are three points to be made in response to these questions. First, the nature of health care, its diffuse and complicated structure, its plethora of competing aims and objectives, is such that it is simply too big and too complex for all decisions to be subject to the depth of investigation which might ensure an optimal deployment of resources. The costs would be too great and the timescale impracticable. Second, while the pursuit of operational efficiency, i.e. ensuring that given objectives are met at least cost, is an important aspect of decision-making in resource allocation whatever the firm, industry or service being considered, it is not a sufficient goal in itself. The other, and at least as important, aspect is that of allocative efficiency, that is, ensuring that what is done is worth doing – in the context of opportunity cost, i.e. that no greater benefit could be provided elsewhere with the same resources. Third, if it is solely individual policy issues (for example, should we have a body scanner?) which are explored, the broad objectives of the National Health Service may never come into focus.

Programme budgeting assists in coming to grips with, or to some extent circumventing, these problems. By beginning with a structure of relatively few programmes, which are directly related to broad health-care objectives, the problems of size and complexity are overcome, the need to keep the objectives of the service in mind is established and the relative priorities to be attached to these objectives are kept to the forefront. While such a framework leaves a gap between an ideal and a practicable approach it is inevitably the latter for which we must settle.

It would of course be desirable to be able to relate the resources involved in different programmes to the final outputs of the programmes in terms of reduced mortality and morbidity and increased comfort and care. While there is an expanding interest in several disciplines in the measurement of health output, knowledge of the production functions of health care – the relationship between the inputs to a particular care regime (medical and nursing manpower, support services, laboratory tests, etc.) and the outputs in terms of improved health – is limited. The reasons for this are several but perhaps the main one is that it is only relatively recently that randomised controlled trials have become accepted. Through trials such as Cochrane [6] discussed, it is possible to assess what the impact or effect of a particular treatment regime is in quantified terms. But the majority of treatment regimes which comprise the health service have not been subject to such studies. This does not mean that these regimes are not effective, simply that the quantified impact is not known. (Given the critical importance of opportunity costs it is not enough to know that a treatment is beneficial; accurate judgements on an optimal resource allocation require quantified evidence on outputs which can be compared for alternative uses of resources.)

Even if these difficulties could be overcome, to measure the production functions as comprehensively as is desirable is a mammoth task. Nevertheless, there is a very strong case for developing the not inconsiderable work already begun. But in the meantime there is a need to settle for something less. 'Intermediate' measures of output do exist; they consist of utilisation or activity data such as discharges, bed utilisation and visits by community services and attendances at clinics or surgeries. While they are perhaps related as much to inputs as to outputs progress can be made with them, as has been recognised by the DHSS in its promotion of 'performance indicators', particularly if the issues of effectiveness are always recognised and can be subjectively judged by experts. This combination can provide a suitable base on which to build the output side of the programme budget. (In chapter 5 the details are provided of how programme budgets were determined for a Scottish health board and some examples of the budgets are presented.)

The nature of programme budgeting

A few points about the nature of programme budgeting are worth emphasising. First, since programme budgeting is intended to provide data relevant to 'broad-brush' planning it is not necessary to present precise details on the budgets. Broad-brush data are sufficient because no detailed, precise plans are expected to emerge at this level. Programme budgeting is a planning framework which can influence the decision-makers not only to take an overview of the health services generally, but to take an overview which relates to broad health-care goals. It is not an evaluative technique. Second, the structure of the budgets should be output orientated in terms of realistic, even if not quantifiable, health-care objectives. There is no single correct way of structuring the budgets; indeed, the classification should vary according to the nature of the trade-offs to be made. The most likely choices in health care are client groups (the elderly, children, mentally ill, etc.) – the structure adopted in chapter 5; disease groups (digestive system diseases, neoplasms, etc.); and geographical groupings (for example, the Resource Allocation Working Party Report [16] was concerned with equity between geographical regions and the 'programme structure' in this instance was, therefore, regionally based). Again, if programme budgeting (or perhaps more accurately 'sub-programme budgeting') is used within an individual programme then appropriate sub-programmes can be devised (for example, for maternity these could be antenatal, labour/birth and postnatal).

   Third, the presentation of the programme budgeting data takes three forms for three related purposes:

(1) The current deployment of resources across the programme heads. This provides a 'snapshot' of how a board or authority's resources are presently being devoted to the different groups and hence to different objectives.
(2) Past trends up to the present position. These indicate how the programmes got to where they are, the growth paths of resources and outputs and, by deduction, the extent to which board or authority policies in the past have affected development. Thus, the study of trends gives an opportunity for monitoring and, once the programme budgeting approach is established, a means of checking fairly quickly whether what was intended has been occurring.
(3) Lastly, future planning. Various scenarios related to the different programmes can be presented, indicating within the expected constraints of future budgeting allocations what possible policies might be pursued for and between different programmes and what the resource and output impacts of these are likely to be.

In this way the programme budgeting provides a planning framework which in no way tells a board or authority what its objectives or priorities ought to be but rather provides some of the essential information on which these objectives and priorities ought to be based. It provides insights rather than policy recommendations. It can allow boards or authorities to form initial judgements about possible imbalances within their present, and recent past, policy and resources decisions and it can allow them to plan better for the future in terms of broad health-care-orientated objectives and priorities. The same considerations of course apply if programme budgeting is used by individual programme-planning groups or health-care planning teams.

While it is possible to overstate the case for programme budgeting, one of its essential ingredients is often underplayed in health-care policy-making – namely, the need for an overview. It is perhaps inevitable that busy administrators seldom have the time to sit back and consider some of the wider implications of their policy-making. Of course, boards and authorities, and their senior officers, will always have some picture at the back of their minds of the direction in which they want the service to move over the next few years but they may not all have the same picture.

The growing pressure from national departments of health for boards or authorities to produce costed strategic plans which can be monitored and the advent of performance reviews means that people will increasingly have to discuss their views and achieve a consensus. The great value of programme budgeting lies in providing data in a particular format which can persuade people to consider policy questions within that format. Discussion is then more likely to centre around common and identifiable trade-offs, and valuation of options then becomes more explicit. This is perhaps the most important contribution of programme budgeting.

This point can be stated in slightly different terms. Without programme budgeting, decisions tend to be made in terms of single issues related to very specific health (or ill-health) questions, for example, we need more psychogeriatric beds (see the Timbury Report [63]) or the perinatal mortality rate is too high (a good example of this being reflected in the Baird Report in Northern Ireland [22]). With programme budgeting prior judgements would be made about the relative priorities to be given to, say, acute medical care and maternity care. Thereafter, given this wider overview, it becomes easier to form judgements about the relative merits of these proposals and their merits *vis-à-vis* other competitors. Given such judgements, further judgements can then be made on whether, if resources are to be made available, these should be at the expense of other programmes or be judged on the basis of the competition for resources *within* the programme concerned.

It perhaps needs to be emphasised that there is no suggestion here that costs alone should determine policy. It is a matter of ensuring that the balance of resources is about right. Just as it may be desirable to introduce a kidney unit to improve the health of one section of the community, so by ensuring in opportunity cost terms that resources generally are being used effectively, the overall health of the community can also be increased. The use of cost data in policy-making is of course not new. What perhaps is not as frequently recognised as it might be is the gap between the extent to which discussion of resources currently affects policy-making and the extent to which it should do so.

What also needs to be recognised is the true relevance of costs in an economic sense. The real importance of cost data and of examination of resource deployment lies in the two issues of efficiency: operational efficiency and allocative efficiency. If resources are used inefficiently in the sense that similar outputs could be achieved at lower cost or using fewer or cheaper resources then there is a loss to the nation in terms of health. This arises because resources which could be freed to provide more services or new services are tied up in pursuing policies which could be achieved in a cheaper way. Thus the price of this inefficiency is less health.

But operational inefficiency is only one aspect of health-service management which can lead to a loss in health. It is also necessary to try to ensure that resources are being deployed across different services and objectives as well as possible. Allocative efficiency relates to 'worthwhileness' and is therefore concerned with the value attached to different uses of resources. It raises issues such as relative priorities attaching to different policies and services or the relative values of the outputs obtained, etc. In other words it poses such questions as how beneficial is this service? Would it be better to expand this programme at the expense of another? Thus, as with operational inefficiency, allocative inefficiency must lead to less health.

Programme budgeting is concerned with both forms of efficiency but it is on allocative efficiency that the main emphasis lies and where its principal innovative role exists. It also appears that much more weight is currently attached to the question of operational efficiency in the health service and that of allocative efficiency is often given much less attention. In that programme budgeting provides a broad planning framework for the consideration of priorities it tends to assist decision-makers in examining issues of relative worthwhileness and hence questions of allocative efficiency. But it must be emphasised that it does so as an information base and not as an evaluative technique. While it can point directions for policy to pursue, the choice of directions, and the weights attached to different options must necessarily come from the application of other analytical and evaluative techniques or from the decision-makers' own values. But the *type* of framework presented by programme budgeting is important because as Pole [52] suggests, it can persuade and assist decision-makers to think about issues in a particular format and to form policy judgements in ways which are most relevant to broad health care policy.

At the same time there is a danger in programme budgeting of 'tramlining'. Just as programme budgeting opens one door in presenting existing data in a particular structure so it may close others in that there may be too much emphasis placed on this new structuring of data. Of course it is possible to present a number of programme budgeting structures but such variety is costly. (Some readers or managers may, indeed, ask for a cost–benefit study of programme budgeting structures.)

The authors believe from their own experience that perhaps the best format is a combination of client-group and disease-group budgets since this would appear to cover the majority of decisions where programme budgeting could help. There is no easy answer to this question of tramlining; however, it is some defence to point out that, given the costs of data presentations within any planning structure, tramlining inevitably exists whatever the data presentations involved. The alternative, of no data presentation, is impossible because everyone who contributes to the discussion adds data of his own! The crucial point is that the tramlines should be those most relevant to the choices to be made.

Conclusion

This chapter has outlined the approach and nature of programme budgeting. It is clear that the nature and organisation of health care is extremely complex and a means of providing an overview, within which broad objectives and priorities for health care can begin to be debated, is desirable. Programme budgeting can provide such a framework of planning.

3

A Framework for Evaluation

Chapter 2 has outlined a means of handling and presenting data which will help planners in making policy choices.

The next stage in the planning process is to begin to look at the mechanisms for evaluation both within and between programmes. Individual options, for example on how to treat particular diseases, can be approached through cost–effectiveness analysis; decisions on whether to treat and, if so, how much to treat of a particular problem can be assisted with the application of cost–benefit analysis. Both these evaluative techniques, which are outlined in more detail in the next chapter, can be costly and time-consuming to apply. It becomes evident very quickly that it is simply not possible to apply such techniques to all the possible options within the particular programmes selected from programme budgeting for more detailed investigation. It will therefore always be a matter of judgement to decide when to apply cost–benefit and cost–effectiveness techniques and in what detail. However, there is a step between programme budgeting and detailed comprehensive application of these evaluative techniques which can often allow 'screening' of options (using screening in its proper sense of the rapid application of simple tests which separate out those people or factors which merit further, more precise, investigation from those people or factors which do not). It is to this evaluative framework that attention now turns. (Some of the presentation in this and the next chapter is based in part on an earlier publication by one of the authors [46].)

In essence it is part of the 'homing in' process begun with programme budgeting and provides the link between programme budgeting and the more explicit evaluation by cost–effectiveness and cost–benefit studies. (Readers already familiar with the cost–

benefit approach will appreciate that the framework for evaluation outlined in this chapter is firmly based in cost–benefit analysis.) Although this chapter concentrates on intra-programme considerations the approach outlined is also applicable at the inter-programme level.

Alternative patterns of care within programmes

One way of looking at the question of alternative patterns of care in any programme is to try to determine what the needs of the relevant population are, set specific standards to meet such needs and thereafter let the balance of care be determined by these two sets of factors.

For example, in care of the elderly it might be discovered through a survey of the elderly population in a particular area that 2 per cent are incontinent. It might then be argued, in terms of specific standards of care, that incontinent individuals ought not to be cared for in their own homes. It might also be argued that residential homes are not staffed or designed to cope with problems of incontinence. It therefore follows that incontinence is deemed to require hospital care and, hence, on the basis of this condition alone the provision of hospital beds for the elderly would need to be at least sufficient to take all those elderly who are incontinent. Again it might be discovered that 2.5 per cent of the elderly living alone in the community are mentally confused. If it is felt that such individuals require a level of care which at least allows them easy and quick access to some means of attention, then it could be argued that all of such individuals should be in sheltered housing. Thus again such an approach could provide a mechanism for determining a minimum level of provision of sheltered housing.

In maternity care, standards can be set related to various levels of risk of complications arising which will determine whether or not it is 'safe' for women to have their babies in a general practitioner unit or whether their confinement should be in a specialist maternity unit. For example, it might be stated that all first pregnancies, all pregnancies where the woman is over a certain age, or where particular complications arose with a previous birth, should be confined in a specialist unit.

This approach of first defining need, second setting some minimum standard to meet this need but third tending to ignore resource considerations is a fairly common practice in health care. However, there are a number of problems associated with each component.

Defining need

The definition of need is fraught with difficulties. As Cooper [7] has remarked 'need is in the eye of the beholder'. Bradshaw [3] described four types of need which reflect a combination of whose values are used and the relationship to use of services; his and other attempts to define need for health care have been critically dissected by Williams [72]. The issue of 'whose values' to use was touched on in the introduction and the conclusion reached that, while the consumers' views should in theory be paramount, in practice health consumers do not have sufficient knowledge to form a generalised view of need which can be used in planning for a group of people. Of course, each individual has a view of what he wants which must be allowed for at the point of consumption of services once they have been offered. If no allowance is made for this, variations may arise between what is planned for on the basis of group needs and what is actually used. Thus if, as suggested above, the needs of the incontinent elderly were defined as requiring institutional care, then those elderly who exercised their rights to remain in their own homes or whose relatives felt able to cope would not move to institutional care and consequently there would be overprovision of institutional accommodation.

For planning purposes there are greater difficulties with the concept of need than that not all consumers will necessarily take what has been provided for them on the basis of a group view of 'need'. In practice, while attempts have been made to incorporate the views of consumers, the most commonly used definition of need is the professional judgement that if there is a treatable condition then a need for care exists. From this definition measurements can be made of 'met' and 'unmet' needs and objectives for care are then derived according to ways of closing the gap between the two measurements. The two fundamental criticisms of this approach are that first it ignores the reality that there are different intensities of need for any one treatment and second it is implied that all need can be met. Thus any one amount of met or unmet need in a population contains a range of severity and, potentially therefore, of benefit from treatment. In clinical practice, the ranking of intensity of need and of implied benefit from care is an integral part of daily work; in deciding which types of patients or clients to treat immediately, which to defer and which not to treat (because he has insufficient resources to do everything) a clinician is in effect defining the *relative* needs of the range of people who could benefit from his services. It is interesting however that, when it comes to planning, the relativity of need is so often ignored and, instead, absolute amounts of implied total benefit are defined. It is, perhaps, a reflection of the same idealistic misconception inherent in the original NHS, namely the belief that there was a finite amount of sickness which could be removed and the only question at issue was the length of time, based on annual amounts of resources made available, required to achieve total health. The consequent difficulty for planners is that, without knowledge of relative benefits within a total there is no way of choosing which of the needy, or potential beneficiaries, should have first claim on limited resources - nor, sometimes, of choosing which types of services to provide, far less how much of each service. In other words, such an approach which denies the logic of choice is not well placed to help in sorting out priorities.

In fairness to those whose task it is to define need as a basis for planning programmes of care, some programmes lend themselves more easily than others to the recognition and acceptance of varying degrees of need. The definition of 'high-risk' groups is common practice and relatively easy when there is reliable information about discrete variations in the probability of disease or disability. It is less easy when these probabilities are on a continuous curve and there is no obvious 'cut-off' point.

For example, in maternity care, over a certain range of ages, the older a woman is so the risk of complications in pregnancy gradually increases. There is thus no particular age at which the risk of complications increases very suddenly. It is therefore necessary, in forming a judgement about the age at which women should be confined in specialist units as opposed to GP units, and in the absence of resource considerations, either to have an arbitrary cut-off age or to argue simply that *all* babies should be delivered in specialist units.

The issue of whose values to use in defining need has been mentioned. A further, quite separate, issue is the fact that each valuer's definitions and valuations of need change over time as he gains new knowledge or experience. Thus given the recognition that need is a dynamic concept, in the time-span of most operational programme plans the criteria of need will change and, in this sense also, there is no 'absolute' amount of need within any particular programme.

Standards of care

Given these difficulties with the concept of need, it is not surprising that problems arise in determining how to meet need in the sense of laying down standards for care. Very often little is known about the effectiveness of different forms of care and this adds to the problems of deciding what type of care and at what level to provide. To use our original example, while it may be ideal (at least in the minds of decision-makers who define need and set standards or care) to propose that all incontinent elderly should be in hospital, presumably such decision-makers would agree that, although not ideal, it is better that such people should be in residential homes rather than, say, living alone in the community. Presumably it would also be agreed by such decision-makers that if the incontinent elderly either have to or want to live alone in the community they should be provided with good support services, for example from the district nurse. Thus even with just one particular type of need there are different levels of care which might go to meet this need to varying extents. With a blanket concept of need and a blanket concept of standard-setting there is a danger that little or no consideration is given to the *relative* strengths of different services or care location in meeting need.

In practice, there is a tendency when planning programmes of care not to set out optional standards but rather to assume that the most advanced – and, hence, assumed to be best – facilities or techniques will give the greatest benefit and are therefore the only and absolute standard to aim for. As in the case of need, this tendency is understandable given the inherent philosophy in health care of trying constantly to improve the quality and effectiveness of care. Again as with need, the constraints of resources are recognised, even if not always accurately, and accommodated in deciding the feasible standard of care in daily clinical work but tend to recede from view when discussing possible future activities.

Thus, while setting absolute levels of need or of quality of care may be a valid approach for the health professions in knowing what is desirable (even although these levels will and should change over time), it is of little value to a health board or programme planning team which has to select from a range of alternatives not only the most desirable direction but also the most efficient and effective mix of activities.

Costs

The most noteworthy omission from the usual approach to questions of balance of care in defining operational pans for meeting needs and standards of care is the lack of consideration of costs or resource use (see, for example, SHAPE [62]). Thus judgements may be formed about the standards of care required to meet different needs without due consideration being given to the costs involved in meeting the standards. Given this omission it is not surprising that programme plans may indicate that there is a large element of unmet need, that a raising of existing standards and therefore provision of more and better facilities are required, but that, in practice, there simply are not sufficient resources for all the need-determined standards to be met. If this occurs, and no thought has been given to either relative priorities or relative costs, it becomes extremely difficult for either the board or the programme planners to judge which needs should be met and which left unmet. The information presented may be so scanty that it is not possible to rethink either the services proposed, in terms of defining alternative standards, or the relative priorities associated with meeting different needs or parts of these needs. The selection of what is feasible within the resources available is then made without any knowledge of the opportunity costs involved and the time spent in devising a single plan – itself a not inconsiderable cost – may have little if any impact on improving the overall health state of the population concerned.

Bringing in cost also highlights the fact the priority attached to meeting a particular need is not just a function of the importance placed on meeting that need. It is also a function of cost, of opportunity costs in terms of the benefits forgone in not being able to meet other needs.

Conclusion

In summary, the approach of defining need and then setting standards of care to meet this need is bedevilled by the scarcity of resources, the difficulties in defining need, the problems of defining standards when little is known about effectiveness, the problems of meeting (and often only partially meeting) some needs as opposed to others and trying to ensure value for money in an opportunity cost context. While many of these problems are not capable of being overcome without mounting sizeable research studies the next section outlines an approach to evaluation that alleviates at least some of these difficulties. In chapter 6 the practicability of the approach is discussed in the context of care of the elderly but it is argued that even where, for example because of data difficulties, its practical application may prove difficult, the general *philosophy* underlying the approach is itself of immense importance to planning and evaluation in health care.

Evaluation framework of marginal analysis

The major change of emphasis in the approach of marginal analysis, when considering alternative patterns of care, is that it starts from a wholly factual base: the fact that resources are scarce. There is a finite limit to the resources available to, and likely to be made available to, the health service. Within the health service, there is again a finite limit to the resources available to, and likely to be made available to, any particular programme. The approach thus immediately moves away from the question of attempting to define total need and concentrates on the following questions in a model of patterns of care:

(1) Given the existing resources available for a particular programme, could some redeployment of these resources result in an increased total benefit from the programme?

(2) If additional resources were made available to the programme, how best could these be deployed to ensure the greatest possible increase in benefit from the programme?

(3) If resources for the programme were to be reduced, how best could cuts be made to ensure the minimum loss in benefit from the programme?

It will become obvious that, in practice, it is not normally possible to answer all these questions in the kind of detailed systematic and quantified fashion that would be ideal. None the less it is important that the right questions are posed rather than perhaps providing answers to wrong questions.

In any programme it will be possible to examine the component parts between which a balance is to be struck. Thus, in maternity, the component parts might be seen either as antenatal care, labour/birth and postnatal care or, alternatively, as community care, GP unit care and specialist unit care. Each of these sub-programmes can be viewed as an entity in itself competing with the other sub-programmes for the limited resources available for the programme as a whole. There will be various costs and benefits associated with each of these sub-programmes and, given a total budget constraint for the programme, the objective of planning will be to make the most of the resources available by deploying them across the sub-programmes in such a way as to maximise the benefit of the programme as a whole. This is achieved when no switching of resources from one sub-programme to another will result in an increase in total benefit from the total programme.

In essence, therefore, the approach looks at balance of care in an opportunity cost context that is that resources will be moved to sub-programme A from sub-programme B if by so doing the increase in benefit in A is greater than the loss of benefit in B. It is by looking at the effect of resource shifts between sub-programmes that the best pattern of care is reached. Note that there is no consideration of setting standards of care. Balance of provision of care in different sub-programmes is determined endogenously by the relative costs and benefits in the various sub-programmes rather than exogenously as in the approach of defining needs to be met and setting standards to meet these needs.

Now it is likely that in any service or sub-programme that is examined, some attempt will already be being made to get as much benefit from the service as possible. Thus as a service is expanded, if the service is organised on a rational basis, it is to be expected that the benefit provided by each additional unit will fall (that is, there will be a 'diminishing marginal benefit'. See Williams and Anderson [73].) This is shown diagrammatically in Figure 3.1.

If the service is operating at the level OQ_1, for each unit of the service the amount of benefit provided will be equal to or greater than OB. If the amount of the service is to be reduced by one unit, then clearly the unit to cut is the last one, which is the Q_1th unit itself. To take out any other unit would mean removing a unit (a visit, for example) which provided a higher level of benefit than that provided by the Q_1th unit. If the service were to be expanded by, say, 10 units, then the selection of what was to be done with these additional units should be based on which of the possible ways of using each additional unit would yield the highest benefit. (In Figure 3.1 these would be the 10 units immediately to the right of Q_1.) If the cost of providing the service were zero, then the optimum level of the service would be OQ_2, the Q_2th unit being the last one which provides any positive benefit at all.

In practice, within any individual service, it is possible that it is not organised quite as rationally as the above would suggest. None the less with an individual service where decision-making on deployment of resources will be in the hands of a single individual

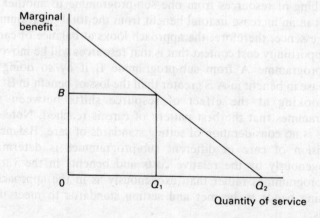

FIGURE 3.1 *Diminishing marginal benefit*

or a small group who are familiar with that particular service and the objectives it is trying to meet, it is likely that the decision-maker(s) will operate their service approximately in these terms. The real problems arise when different services with different unit costs, different benefits and different managers have to be brought together to obtain as great a benefit as possible from the combined services (that is, to establish the best pattern of care for a programme).

In a programme with two sub-programmes (although the principles outlined apply no matter how many sub-programmes there are) where the balance of care between the two sub-programmes is to be considered, the objective will be to try to ensure that the levels of the two sub-programmes are pitched such that no switch of resources between them will result in an overall increase in benefit from the two sub-programmes in combination. This means that the benefit and the cost of the marginal units in each sub-programme should be compared. If it can be shown that the benefit/cost ratio of the last unit currently being produced in sub-programme A is greater than the similar ratio in sub-programme B, then some reduction in B and increase in A will be justified, since it will increase the overall total benefit from the resources available. This process would be continued until the benefit/cost ratio for the last unit produced in each sub-programme is the same, that is, the ratio of the marginal benefit to the marginal cost is equal in each.

A numerical example will help to illustrate this. Assume that the two sub-programmes have benefits and costs as in Table 3.1. (For ease of exposition it is assumed that marginal cost is constant in each sub-programme. In practice this may well not be the case but the underlying principles remain.) If it were possible to measure all costs and benefits in money terms, as Table 3.1 and Figure 3.2 imply, many of the problems of health-care planning would be much reduced. Since it is not, then difficulties remain. Thus while this numerical example implies knowledge which is not normally available, it is the thinking behind the process which is important rather than the numbers themselves. Diagrammatically the same data shown in Table 3.1 can be presented as in Figure 3.2.

In sub-programme A, the most that should ever be supplied of this service would be 6 units. This is because the 7th and 8th units each provides a smaller benefit than it costs to produce. Similarly

TABLE 3.1 *Marginal benefits and costs of two sub-programmes*

Unit	Sub-programme A				Sub-programme B			
	Marginal costs £	Total costs £	Marginal benefits £	Total benefits £	Marginal costs £	Total costs £	Marginal benefits £	Total benefits £
1st	10	10	35	35	20	20	60	60
2nd	10	20	30	65	20	40	50	110
3rd	10	30	25	90	20	60	40	150
4th	10	40	20	110	20	80	30	180
5th	10	50	15	125	20	100	20	200
6th	10	60	10	135	20	120	10	210
7th	10	70	5	140	20	140	0	210
8th	10	80	0	140	20	160	0	210

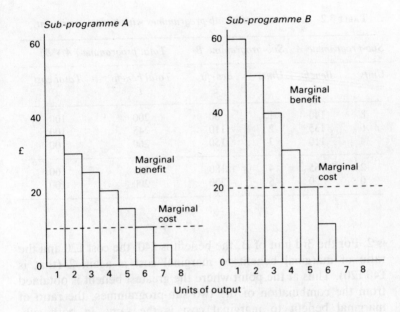

FIGURE 3.2 *Marginal benefits and costs of two sub-programmes*

the maximum number of units which sub-programme B should be asked to produce would be 5. (Put differently, note that the total benefit in A of 8 units is £140 and the total cost is only £80. Since the total benefit exceeds the total costs would it not be justified to produce all 8 units? The answer is no, because the production of both the 7th and 8th units reduces the 'net benefit' (that is benefit minus cost). This serves to indicate the importance of considering marginal benefits and costs.)

Now if the total budget available for this programme were £100, a number of combinations of outputs from A and B are possible, as indicated in Table 3.2. Which combination should be selected? Given an objective to obtain as much benefit as possible from the combined sub-programmes, then the choice would be 4 units of A and 3 of B which for £100 is the combination that yields the highest total benefit (that is £260).

It should be noted (from Table 3.1) that the marginal benefit of producing the 4th unit of A is £20, the marginal cost £10 and therefore the marginal benefit to marginal cost ratio is £20/£10 that

TABLE 3.2   *Combinations of sub-programmes with budget constraint*

Sub-programme A		Sub-programme B		Total programme (A + B)	
Units	Benefit £	Units	Benefit £	Total benefit £	Total cost £
8	140	1	60	200	100
6	135	2	110	245	100
4	110	3	150	260	100
2	65	4	180	245	100
0	0	5	200	200	100

is 2. For the 3rd unit of B, the benefit is £40, the cost £20 and the ratio of marginal benefit to marginal cost is again 2 (that is £40/£20). Thus at the point where the greatest benefit is obtained from the combination of the two sub-programmes, the ratio of marginal benefit to marginal cost is the same in both sub-programmes. This in effect provides the 'decision rule' for determining the deployment of resources across different sub-programmes no matter how many there may be, that is the point at which maximum benefit is achieved from a given budget is where for each sub-programme the ratio of marginal benefit to marginal cost is the same. This rule is of central importance in considering the issue of alternative patterns of care. (For a diagrammatic and more detailed outline of the approach see the appendix to this chapter.)

One of the great strengths of this approach is that it does not require estimates to be made of total costs, total benefits or total needs. It is marginal costs and marginal benefits on which the approach rests.

It might appear, however, that the approach can only operate, as indicated above, if marginal costs and marginal benefits are measurable. In many instances where patterns of care are being considered – balance of care of the elderly between the community, sheltered housing, residential home and hospital; the pattern of maternity care with varying emphases on antenatal, labour/birth and postnatal care; the mix of cancer services between health education, screening and curative; etc. – fairly good estimates can be made of the costs and, in particular, the marginal costs. Benefits are normally much more difficult to estimate and value.

But judgements have to be made about the benefits of different services and programmes, *whatever* approach to evaluation is used. In the numerical example outlined on p. 28, the marginal costs in sub-programme B are twice those in A. If no monetary values are available for the benefits, the optimal distribution of resources between the two sub-programmes would be obtained when a *judgement* was reached that the marginal benefit in B was twice that in A (and the budget was consumed). Thus unless or until some of the very difficult issues of benefit measurement are solved, the use of the marginal analysis approach will be dependent on the judgement of decision-makers about the relative magnitude of marginal benefits. What is important is that the judgements being exercised would then be about the right issues, that is the *marginal* benefits.

Some studies using this type of approach, for example in the balance of care of the elderly, have been published [27, 67]. Thus in forming judgements about alternative patterns of care for the elderly – domiciliary care, sheltered housing, residential home and hospital – what is required is to obtain estimates of the relevant marginal costs and form judgements about the relative values of the relevant marginal benefits.

For example, in deciding about the balance between residential home places and geriatric beds, estimates can be made of the cost of providing additional residential home places to be filled by current geriatric patients, the resource savings on the hospital side and, at the least, a description of the patients likely to be involved in such a move from hospital to residential home. Similarly estimates can be made of the cost of providing additional hospital beds to be filled by residents of residential homes, the resource saving on the residential home side and a description of the residents likely to be involved in such a move from residential home to hospital. Thereafter in deciding upon the optimal balance between residential home places and geriatric beds, judgements about relative benefits for the individuals likely to be affected would have to be made and compared with the costs of making the changes. The equating of the ratios of marginal benefit to marginal cost would then come into play.

The important points to be drawn from this are:

(1) the determination of the boundary of care – and hence the balance of care – is a function of the relative costs and benefits of care in the different locations; and

(2) to determine the balance of care it is not necessary to determine the costs and benefits of care for all individuals but merely those likely to be affected by small shifts in the existing boundaries of care, that is those of relatively high dependency levels in residential homes and those of relatively low dependency levels in hospital.

For the present it is assumed that the question of benefit measurement has to be based on the judgements of the decision-makers and *to this extent* the approach outlined does not differ from the processes involved in present decision-making in health care. But there are important differences. First, judgements are to be made against a background of the costs of alternative policies and, most important, the *marginal* costs. Secondly, in so far as judgements about benefits have to be made these do not have to be made about total benefits but only *marginal* benefits. Thirdly, the approach, by providing data about the characteristics of the people (or care) likely to be affected, allows decision-makers to make more informed judgements.

Thus, in the care of the elderly example above, cost data can be provided on the care of the individuals close to the existing boundaries of care and by surveying such individuals a picture of their characteristics (in such terms as dependence and disability) can be built up. By presenting cost data, not only on the margins between residential home and hospital but also on other margins relevant to care of the elderly, such as own home/sheltered housing, the relative costs of shifting these different boundaries of care can be seen against informed judgements of the likely effects.

Clearly the approach is not restricted to obtaining the best balance of care with existing resources. It can just as easily be used to indicate what new balance of care would be desirable should there be an increase or a decrease in the resources available to a particular programme.

As outlined thus far the approach assumes no *qualitative* changes within particular sub-programmes. It is concerned solely with quantitative changes in the balance of care between existing types of sub-programmes. However, it need not be constrained in this way.

For example, in care of the elderly a case might be made for some 'half-way' house between the existing form of residential care, with largely unqualified staff, and geriatric hospital care. Such 'nursing home' accommodation might be proposed for those very frail and dependent elderly in residential homes and/or for those in hospital who, among the hospitalised elderly, are relatively independent.

The approach can accommodate a new form of care or a shift in quality of an existing form of care in the determination of the optimum balance of care provided that:

(a) data can be obtained on the costs of the new form of care (in this example nursing home accommodation) and on the characteristics of those currently in both residential homes and hospital who might be moved to such nursing home accommodation; and

(b) decision-makers can again make judgements about the relative benefits for such individuals in the different care locations.

Summary

This approach of 'marginal analysis' provides a useful evaluative framework for examining questions of alternative patterns of care. It avoids the question of measurement of total need and thus offers an alternative both to those who believe that such measurement is conceptually irrelevant, and to those who believe that it is extremely difficult and/or costly. It concentrates initially on the fact that there are limited resources available both to the health service as a whole and to individual programmes within health care. It does not *solve* the question of benefit measurement but, by providing cost data on care, and offering descriptions of the effects of relatively small changes in the supply of services, it highlights the nature of trade-offs which is essential in any planning of alternative patterns of care.

The use of this approach is such that it leaves much to the judgements of the decision-maker. It provides estimates of the implications of redeploying resources within, to or from a programme where alternative patterns of care are possible. The decision-maker is left to judge the relative effectiveness of different forms of care and the relative values attaching to them at the margin but the framework is created to allow him to see the opportunity costs involved in the different options between which he has to choose. That is no small benefit.

Appendix

This appendix sets out the approach of marginal analysis in diagrammatic form.

Assume that the issue to hand is the balance of care between hostels for the mentally handicapped and hospital care and further assume initially that both costs and benefits are measurable in money terms.

For residents of both the hostels and hospital there will be a range of dependency stretching from low to high. The distribution of the hostels and hospital populations might therefore be as in Figure A3.1. In (a) it is assumed that all the mentally handicapped in hospital are more dependent than those in hostels. In (b) it is assumed that there is some overlap of dependence and hence overlap of the two curves.

Now if it is also assumed that the cost of care in both institutions increases with dependence then the cost picture emerging for different dependency levels might be depicted as in Figure A3.2.

Now for individuals of dependency levels up to D_1 it is cheaper to care for them in hostels than in hospital; above D_1 it is cheaper to care for them in hospital.

But what about benefit? What the shape of the benefit curves will be with increasing dependence in both hostels and hospital is difficult to judge. However, it is likely that the benefit of being in a hostel will tend to increase with dependence (and with the amount of care given) but may cease to increase above a certain level of dependence when, for example, the nature of care which a hostel can provide ceases to be as appropriate for the patient's condition. For some relatively high levels of dependence it can be assumed from empirical evidence that the benefit of being in hospital is greater than that of being in a hostel. Thus the important consideration is that at *some* level of dependence the hospital benefit curve will be above the hostel benefit curve. This can occur in several ways, as indicated in Figure A3.3.

In a costless world, an individual would move from a hostel to hospital at D_a in Figure A3.3(a), D_b in (b) and D_d in (d). In (c) no

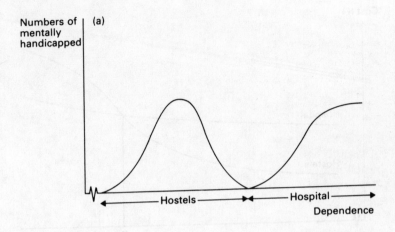

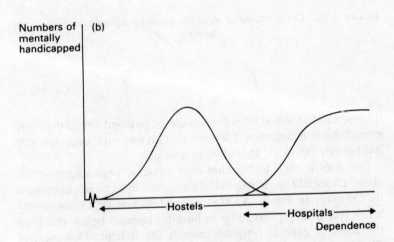

FIGURE A3.1   *Possible population distributions*

one would be in a hostel because the hospital benefit curve is always above the hostel benefit curve.

Introducing costs into Figure A3.3 gives the picture shown in Figure A3.4.

In each of (a) to (d) in Figure A3.4 for dependency levels less than D_1 the benefits of being in a hostel are greater than the costs; above D_1 the costs exceed the benefits. Since one basic tenet which

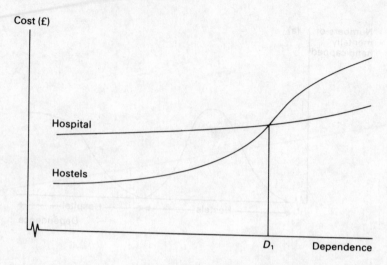

Cost (£)

Hospital

Hostels

D_1 Dependence

FIGURE A3.2   *Costs related to different levels of dependence: hostels and hospitals*

is subscribed to is that no policy should be pursued where the costs exceed the benefits, then it follows that no one with a dependency level greater than D_1 should be in a hostel.

But does it then follow that only those of dependency levels above D_1 should be in hospital? The answer must be not necessarily. Certainly in Figure A3.4(a) and (b) no one with dependency levels less than D_2 should be in hospital because below this level the costs of care in hospital exceeds the benefit. However, in Figure A3.4(a) and (b) for those of dependency levels between D_2 and D_1, in both hospital and hostels benefits exceed costs. In Figure A3.4(c) and (d) benefits exceed costs in hospital for all levels of dependence and in hostels for all levels of dependence up to D_1. The dividing line separating those who are to be in hospital from those who are to be in hostels is determined by the marginal benefit/marginal cost rule, that is, the boundary line falls where the ratio of marginal benefit to marginal cost is equal in both hostels and hospital. In Figure A3.4(a), for example, this occurs at D_3 where

37

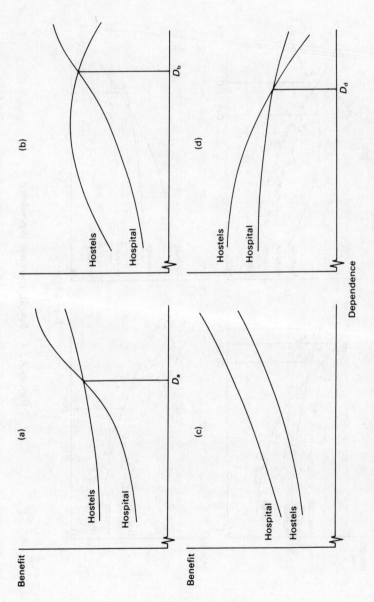

FIGURE A3.3 *Benefit curves and dependence: hostels and hospitals*

38

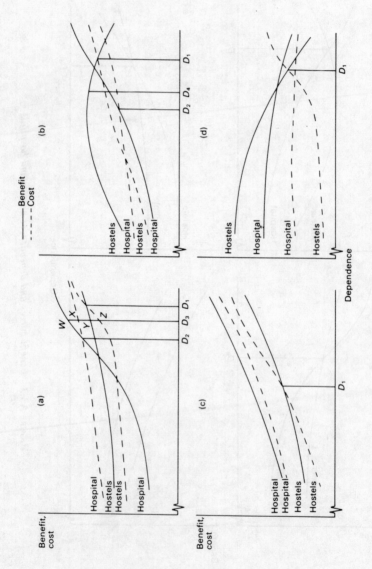

FIGURE A3.4 *Benefit, costs and dependence*

$$\frac{WD_3}{XD_3} = \frac{YD_3}{ZD_3}$$

(In practice the shapes of the relevant benefit curves are much more likely to be as in (a) and (b) than in (c) or (d).)

The important points to be drawn from this are:

(1) the determination of the boundary of care – and hence the balance of care – is a function of the relative marginal costs and benefits of care in the different locations; and

(2) to determine the balance of care it is not necessary to determine the cost and benefits of care for all individuals but merely those likely to be affected by small shifts in the existing boundaries of care, that is those of relatively high dependency levels in hostels and those of relatively low dependency levels in hospital.

Thus if in Figure A3.4(b) it was assumed that the existing boundary of care was at D_4, then in trying to decide whether this was the optimum, an examination would be required of the costs and benefits of those (in hostels currently) with dependency levels just below D_4 that is those in the hostels who are most dependent and of those (in hospital currently) with dependency levels just above D_4 that is those in the hospital who are least dependent.

The fact that at present it is seldom possible to place monetary values on health-care benefit means that it is not possible simply to fit the appropriate numbers to the marginal benefit/marginal cost ratios and expect a decision to emerge. What marginal analysis provides is the relevant framework for the exercise of judgement about the relative benefits of different programmes of sub-programmes *at the margin* and thereafter for a judgement to be made about the relative size of the marginal benefit/marginal cost ratios.

4

Techniques for Evaluation

In this chapter two specific and related economic techniques of evaluation – cost–effectiveness analysis and cost–benefit analysis – are discussed. Both are important but perform rather different functions. Many studies in health care which claim to be cost–benefit studies are in practice cost–effectiveness studies and it is therefore necessary to delineate clearly between the two approaches lest the unwary reader be misled.

The techniques have a lengthy history in economics and the literature on them (see, for example, Mishan [45] and Sugden and Williams [65]) has expanded markedly in the past few years. But it is only fairly recently that their application in health care has become at all prevalent. (See, for some examples, Drummond [25].) Even now the number of good studies using these techniques remains relatively small. This chapter outlines the theory and concepts of the approaches. Some applications are presented in chapter 7 to allow the reader to understand better how to apply the techniques to problems which he may face.

Cost–effectiveness analysis

The approach

Cost–effectiveness analysis is essentially concerned with the 'how' of policy. It can assist in decisions on the techniques of care delivery. It normally *in itself* provides no assistance in deciding either whether to pursue a particular policy or *how much* of a

40

particular policy to pursue. It is constrained to considerations of how at least cost to meet a particular objective; or, given a fixed budget to meet a particular objective, how best to deploy this budget.

To use cost–effectiveness analysis it is necessary to be able first to answer the questions: What is the objective? What are the possible options? What are the effects of each of the possible options? What are the costs of each of the possible options?

The objective could take various forms. For example, in screening for breast cancer, it might be considered relevant to aim for one or more of the following:

(1) the lowest screening cost per woman screened; *← Not*
(2) the lowest screening cost per positive case detected;
(3) the lowest cost, including treatment and screening costs, per positive case detected; *✗ Treatment not included.*
(4) the lowest cost, including treatment and screening costs, per true positive case detected;
(5) the lowest cost, including treatment and screening costs, per death averted;
(6) the lowest cost, including treatment and screening costs, per year of life extended; or
(7) the lowest cost, including treatment and screening costs and allowing for savings in treatment costs for cases which would have presented symptomatically, per year of life extended.

This list could be extended and made even more complex. However, it serves to indicate that the specification of the objective *in some detail* is important in cost–effectiveness analysis. To have a simple objective, as in (1) above, might result in a very different policy from one which pursued more complicated objectives such as (6) or (7). In some instances it may be that the final definition of the objective will be dependent on the cost–effectiveness study itself. For example, different screening techniques may result in different rates of false positives which, in turn, could affect the objectives. Thus it may be that a final choice of objectives can only be made if objectives are initially set in terms of both true and total positive cases detected, and cost–effectiveness studies are mounted on the basis of each of these objectives;

judgement can then be made as to which of the objectives is to be preferred.

The cost–effectiveness analyst would tend to be suspicious about the first objective above, that is, to achieve the lowest possible screening cost per woman screened. Suspicions would arise, first, because of the omission of certain costs (such as time spent at the clinic) which would occur because of screening and might vary with different screening regimes, and second, because of the lack of homogeneity of the 'output' as stated. For example, although cost per woman screened is clearly relevant in deciding what screening policy to pursue, if policy A has a cost per woman screened of £5 and policy B £8, would the chosen option be A if it could also be shown that B yielded twice as many positive cases per 1000 screenings as A and hence that B was cheaper in terms of the cost per *positive* case detected?

Clearly the question of the definition of the objective in cost–effectiveness studies is very important if for no other reason than that absence of a careful initial definition may result in an irrelevant study. Although objectives will tend to vary from study to study two broad guidelines can be suggested. First, the objectives should be couched in as near to 'final outputs' as is possible. Thus, lives prolonged or years of life extended are measures of effectiveness which would normally be preferred to that of women screened. Secondly, in so far as the objectives influence which costs are included, the definition should include as many of the relevant costs as possible. Thus costs of treatment and screening would normally be preferred to costs of screening alone.

Strictly, cost–effectiveness analysis can only cope with a programme in which there is a single output. This is because it cannot deal with different weights to be attached to multiple outputs.

Similar considerations apply in using cost–effectiveness analysis to determine how best to use a fixed budget to meet a particular objective. Again the objective should be defined in as near to 'final outputs' as possible and the defining of costs to be covered by the fixed budget (and of those not) requires careful consideration in setting the objective. However, before discussing the issues of effectiveness and costs in more detail, there is the prime question of which options are to be considered relevant to the study. It may well be that not all possible options are actually included in the study but one of the important features of cost–effectiveness analysis is that as many as possible of the feasible and reasonable options are identified. Only in this way can it be assumed that the most cost–effective option will be chosen. Although this may seem a very obvious point there is some danger that too narrow a selection of options for analysis may result in the study suggesting the provision of a less-than-best policy.

This identification of options is not wholly independent of the first requirement of setting the objective. Indeed it may well be that when possible options are listed some redefining of the objective becomes desirable. For example, some options may also produce other effects which have then, in turn, to be considered for inclusion in the objective.

Turning to the third question, in cost–effectiveness analysis it is necessary to be able to quantify as far as knowledge will permit the effect of the different options. It is not enough to be able to state that a particular option will be beneficial. Because the relative effectiveness of different options has to be compared, it is necessary to be able to quantify the effectiveness of each option. Where such information is not currently available it may then be an integral part of the cost–effectiveness study to mount research to obtain the information.

While it is clearly ideal to be able to measure the effectiveness of all the assembled options this could in some instances be an extremely costly exercise. The research required to obtain the necessary data might result in a lengthy delay before a decision could be reached. On the other hand it may emerge – particularly when cost data are introduced – that sufficient knowledge exists on effectiveness of a particular option to be able to form a quick judgement that, while effectiveness has not been measured with any precision, it is thought to be so low as to make that option clearly inferior to others on the list.

There can be no hard and fast rule about the extent of precision required in the measurement of effectiveness. Good judgement is obviously important on this matter. Provided that it is certain that the most cost-effective solution is not being rejected because of ignorance about its effectiveness then the exercise of judgement is obviously desirable if it can reduce the amount of work involved in the study.

The fourth requirement is to be able to measure the costs associated with each option. Such costs will normally include *all* those costs associated with implementing the option. They ought, therefore, to include not only the costs falling on the NHS budget but also those which would be incurred by other agencies such as social work departments, the patients themselves and the patients' relatives. In some instances the measurement of some costs will be difficult or impossible. For example, if an option involves domiciliary care there may be some 'costs' (such as stress) falling on patients' relatives which will not be quantified or at least not in money terms. None the less, as accurate a description as possible of the nature and extent of such intangible costs should be included in the cost–effectiveness analysis. In this way the decision-maker will know about these costs even if their valuation has to be left to his subjective judgement.

In some instances it may not be strictly necessary even to attempt to measure these intangible costs in a cost–effectiveness study. For example, the costs borne by women attending for breast screening is a relevant cost. Such costs, which would include travel, time, inconvenience and perhaps psychological costs, may be difficult or impossible to quantify. It may well be, however, that for different screening techniques – clinical examination, thermography, mammography – the costs falling on women screened may be the same or at least very similar. When this occurs the addition of a *constant* cost, albeit unquantified, will not affect which policy is selected by cost–effectiveness analysis.

One aspect of costing for cost–effectiveness studies should be emphasised. The costs used must be the costs incurred as a result of implementing the option. This means that care has to be exercised in ensuring that the resources associated with the option are correctly determined and valued. For example, the costs of hospital care may vary depending upon the existing level of bed occupancy. If bed occupancy is 100 per cent, or as close to it as is practical, then the costs of additional hospital care to deal with an option requiring hospital stay would involve either the displacement of existing patients or the creation of additional beds. If bed occupancy is low, say 50 per cent, then the cost of the additional hospital care may be quite low, particularly if staff with the relevant skills are already in post but underemployed.

Another aspect of costing should be noted. In some instances it may be that the option with the least cost per unit of output provides less of the output than do other options. For example option A may provide 100 units of output at a cost of £100, that is £1 per unit of output. Option B may provide 150 units of output at a cost of £450, that is £3 per unit of output. While option A is clearly the more cost–effective it may be that the decision-maker would still have a preference for option B in that it provides a greater output and the costs – at £3 per unit of output – appear still very reasonable for the nature of the output involved. But the relevant figure for the consideration of this question is not £3 per unit of output but £7. This is because the 50 additional (or 'marginal') units cost an extra £350 (that is £450 – £100) which means that these extra units can only be obtained at a cost of £7 unit of output.

If all these questions are answered then the task in the cost–effectiveness analysis involves only a ranking of options in terms of their relative cost–effectiveness. If the objective is fixed in the sense of there being a specified level of output then the ranking from the cost–effectiveness analysis will simply be in terms of the total cost for each option meeting the objective. If the objective is specified in terms of the type of output but not the total quantity then the ranking from cost–effectiveness analysis will be in terms of cost per unit of output for each option. Again if the objective is stated in terms of a fixed budget to obtain some type of output then the ranking will be in terms of the number of units of output obtainable for this budget for each of the options.

Bed sores: a hypothetical example

Many aspects of cost–effectiveness analysis can be exemplified by looking at the issue of bed-sore prevention. The initial objective can be stated as follows: to reduce bed sores at the least cost per bed sore. A number of possible options is available: for example, normal beds with regular turning of the patients by nurses; air beds; water beds; and rocking beds. Each of these has implications for staff time and equipment costs, and for other aspects of the patient's welfare. Each has a particular level of effectiveness for the care of bed sores. It is thus possible to indicate over a particular time period the costs involved in the different options and the effectiveness of each option. Thus the following picture might be established.

TABLE 4.1 *Bed-sore prevention: I*

Option	Costs* £	Effectiveness
A	500	Complete absence of bed sores
B	400	Complete absence of bed sores
C	200	Complete absence of bed sores
D	80	Complete absence of bed sores

* These are the costs involved *in addition to* the other costs of care

Now on the basis of the above the choice, all other things being equal, is option D. Although this is a rather simplistic example there are a number of issues in health care which lend themselves to very straightforward analysis of this type.

However, it may be that there are differentials in the effectiveness of the different options. As a result consideration has to be given to unit costs of care, that is, to how much it costs to eliminate bed sores compared with differing levels of reduction of bed sores. The 'balance sheet' thus becomes related to some unit of output, for example costs per bed sore avoided. An example, based on an initial number of bed sores of 10, is presented in Table 4.2.

TABLE 4.2 *Bed-sore prevention: II*

Option	Costs £	Number of bed sores occurring	Number of bed sores prevented	Average cost per bed sore prevented £
E	600	8	2	300
F	300	6	4	75
G	425	5	5	85
H	900	0	10	90

Now the best option here might appear to be F, since it results in a reduction of 40 per cent (4 out of 10) of bed sores at an average cost of only £75. It is preferable to option E since it results in both fewer bed sores and lower cost.

But options G and H both result in fewer bed sores, although at higher total and average costs. Is option F to be preferred to G or H? Option G is not very expensive at £425 per annum and £85 per bed sore prevented and option H, although relatively expensive, actually *eliminates* bed sores.

In considering option G versus option F, the average cost of £85 per bed sore prevented is *not* the relevant figure. To reduce bed sores per annum from 6 to 5, that is choose option G rather than F, means a cost of £425 as compared with £300. Thus the 'marginal' bed sore avoided costs £125 not £85.

In the same way, comparing option F with H, 6 extra bed sores are avoided at a cost of £600 or £100 per marginal bed sore avoided. Thus, provided that the £900 is available to implement option H, then H is to be preferred to option G, since the marginal cost is lower in H than in G.

The important point, therefore, is to consider *marginal* costs of bed-sore elimination and Table 4.2 can be revamped as shown in Table 4.3.

TABLE 4.3 *Bed-sore prevention: marginal costs*

Option	Number of bed sores prevented	Total cost £	Difference in bed sores prevented	Difference in cost £	Marginal cost £
(1) F	4	300	—	—	—
G	5	425	1	125	125
(2) F	4	300	—	—	—
H	10	900	6	600	100

The questions this raises are:

other than implementing option F, is it worth

(a) implementing option G to prevent one more bed sore at an additional and marginal cost of £125; or

(b) is it worth implementing option H to prevent an additional 6 bed sores at a total additional cost of £600 (as compared with option F) and at a marginal cost of £100.

Cost–effectiveness analysis cannot *answer* these questions but by presenting the data in this form it forces judgements about the option to be selected to be made more explicitly and hence, presumably, to be better.

If, in addition, the question of the benefit to the patient of earlier discharge is introduced then the edifice of cost–effectiveness begins to break down because it is difficult to introduce this element into the above (although it is possible by considering the output not only in terms of bed sores but also shorter hospital stay). When issues of relative worth and value of output emerge then cost–effectiveness analysis, while being of considerable assistance in laying out the framework for discussion of the options, cannot normally show which options to select. This is because, to reiterate, it is concerned with technique and not with questions of relative priorities or values.

If cost–effectiveness analysis is taken in its other context, that is a fixed budget for the reduction of bed sores, then it is easy to see that the data presented above can be used to indicate the best way of using the budget to reduce bed sores. If the budget is fixed *and* the objective is constrained solely to the issue of reducing bed sores, then for such a problem there will normally be a single solution indicating how best to use the budget.

Cost–effectiveness analysis is thus a very useful tool despite its limitations. Indeed the majority of studies in health care which are termed cost–benefit studies frequently transpire to be cost–effectiveness studies. The main benefits which cost-effectiveness analysis can bring to the decision-maker are, first, providing a framework for consideration of options, second, ensuring that the selection of options for consideration is reasonably comprehensive, third, setting out the costs together with measures of effectiveness and, fourth, giving emphasis to *marginal* considerations. What it does not do is to indicate directly whether something is worth doing in cases where there are both positive costs and desired outputs, nor does it show how much to do. These questions require value judgements and values on the benefit side; as such they lie within the province of cost–benefit analysis, which is now considered.

Cost–benefit analysis

The question of whether it is worthwhile pursuing a particular policy is clearly an important issue in health care. Given that the resources available to treat illness and promote health are inevitably limited and the demands made on these resources at times appear insatiable, it follows that some choice has to be exercised in deciding which policies to pursue – and, just as important, which not to pursue. For this type of choice to be made it is desirable to have some evaluative technique which can assist in deciding between competing objectives and not just, as with cost–effectiveness analysis, be able to evaluate alternative ways of reaching some given objective.

To be able to judge the 'worthwhileness' of a particular policy it is necessary to judge whether the gain from pursuing it more than offsets the sacrifice involved. In other words there is a need to weigh the benefits against the costs and this leads into the philosophy and technique of cost–benefit analysis.

As Williams [71] indicates: 'Cost–benefit studies stress the simple truth that the decision whether or not to pursue a particular course of action depends on both costs and benefits.' Bringing these together is the single most important contribution of cost–benefit analysis. While there is a tendency on the part of economists to underplay this point (because, through their training, it appears self-evident) it remains the case that, as Williams [71] continues, 'we see far too many recommendations based on assertions that x is cheaper than y (without adequate consideration of relative benefits) or that x is more effective than y (without adequate consideration of relative costs)'.

Thus by assessing the costs and benefits of different policies, judgements can be formed about the relative worth of committing scarce resources in different ways. While no health care policy should be pursued which results in a greater cost to society than the benefit it bestows on society, it does not automatically follow that all policies which result in a greater benefit than cost can be pursued. Ideally, if cost–benefit analysis were widely applied in health care, those policies that show the greatest benefit per £ of resources used should be given greatest priority. Cost–benefit analysis thus has all the virtues and requirements of cost–effectiveness analysis *plus* the capacity to assist in decisions about 'worthwhileness'.

But what is meant by 'costs' and 'benefits' in cost–benefit analysis? How are these to be measured? Although it can be stated simply that the relevant benefits are those accruing to society at large, the problems of benefit measurement are considerable.

Benefit measurement is one of the major issues involved in cost–benefit analysis in health care and, indeed, in all health-care evaluation. What is meant by better health? How are changes in health status to be measured? How are such changes valued? Whose values are relevant?

The definition of health is itself fraught with difficulty. The World Health Organization [74] has defined health as: 'a state of complete physical, mental and social well being, and not merely the absence of disease or infirmity' but, for considering health measurement and valuation, such a definition is not particularly helpful.

The standpoint adopted in defining health is also important; for example, it can be defined biologically in terms of the functioning of the cells of the body. But again this type of definition is not of much assistance for measuring and valuing health. Yet again health can be seen as a social phenomenon, in terms of social functioning, and this perhaps is moving closer to a type of definition which might allow health to be measured and valued.

If a social definition of health is accepted, then in theory at least it is possible to devise a 'health status index'. (For an example, see the appendix to this chapter.) Such an index would allow measurement of changes in health status not just ordinally in the sense of stating that one health state is better than another, but cardinally in the sense of *how much* better one state is than another.

Two points should be noted. Often to state that an individual's state of health is better than it was may well be a technical judgement that ought to be made by experts, that is, clinicians. To state that a movement of health status from a to b is to be weighted twice as highly as a movement from b to c is clearly value laden and the question of whether *this* judgement should be left to clinicians is very much less certain. The second type of judgement is particularly important because it is from it that the issues of worthwhileness and *monetary* valuation of benefits arise. If a movement in health status from a to b is weighted twice as highly as a movement from b to c, then the implication for resource utilisation is that it is worthwhile devoting up to twice as many resources to achieve the former movement rather than the latter.

In the health service at present measurement and valuation of benefit is occurring *by implication* in almost all decisions on resource allocation. This follows because a decision to implement a particular policy at a cost of £50 000 implies that the benefits of doing so are valued at at least £50 000 (or it would not be done). A decision not to implement that policy implies a judgement that the benefits are valued at less than £50 000.

One measure of 'benefit' which is frequently used is that of cost saving. However, in effect 'cost-saving' is a negative cost (which is of course a good thing) rather than a benefit *per se*. Another frequently found measure of benefit is that of output in terms of contribution to gross national product (GNP). If an individual is ill or dies then his productive capacity may be lost. In so far as his earnings can be taken as a measure of the value of his output, then lost earnings provide an estimate of the cost of illness (assuming the illness prevents the patient from working) or of premature death.

One of the major difficulties with this approach is that while part of the objective of health care is to return people who have been ill to work as quickly as possible this is only a part of the benefit of good health. There are clearly benefits other than capacity to work. Viewed in this way, however, the lost earnings measure provides a 'floor' to the measurement of benefit of health care. Some economists sometimes ingeniously, sometimes naively have attempted to 'allow' for other benefits but these attempts are generally rather suspect. The problems, in this approach, of measuring the benefits of health care to housewives and the elderly, for example, are obvious. If GNP is assumed to be the basis of benefit in health care then the approach can be defended – but it is doubtful if many would subscribe to such a narrow definition of benefit. None the less this is the approach which is most commonly found.

A further approach to benefit measurement starts from the judgement that it is the consumer who should be 'sovereign'. This 'consumer-sovereignty' approach suggests that the people whose preferences are relevant in valuing benefits are the consumers of health care (that is the patients) and/or the potential consumers (that is the community at large). Clearly it would not be practical to ask people – how much would you be prepared to pay to avoid certain death? Nor indeed is this the relevant question.

In terms of *planning* health care the issue revolves around the question of deployment and resources to different types of health care. It is thus concerned with deploying resources to reduce the *risk* of death or illness for groups of individuals. The relevant question, for example for valuing life, then becomes not how much would an individual – plus relatives, friends, etc. – be willing to pay to avoid certain death but rather how much would such a group be prepared to pay to reduce the individual's risk of death from say x to y where both x and y are very much less than one (where one equals certain death).

This question carries more meaning and can be approached by studying individuals' behaviour in conditions of risk. If it is possible to indicate how much individuals are prepared to pay to reduce their risk then this provides a value of the risk reduction. Thus if it could be shown that in a particular situation 10 000 individuals are prepared to pay £1 on average to reduce their risk from 2 in 10 000 to 1 in 10 000, then the 'value of life' (since one life would be saved) would be £10 000.

An alternative, since there are few situations which lend themselves to behavioural analysis of this type, is to present individuals with hypothetical situations and persuade them to trade-off safety and resources. For example, individuals may be faced with the choice of two airlines which differ only in their safety records and the level of their fares.

This approach is still at a developmental stage (see, for example, Jones Lee [37]) but if it is believed that the consumer should be sovereign, then this methodology should be used to derive values for the benefits of health care. Clearly the issue of whether individuals can make the necessary judgements and want to make them is very central to the acceptance and acceptability of this approach.

These two methods are not ideal – the first because at best it only measures a part of the benefits of health care and the second because it is still being developed and may not be acceptable anyway. But this does not mean that nothing can be done. The question of cost savings and of lost earnings are important and relatively easily measured. In addition it is possible to indicate in many instances, given the framework of cost–benefit analysis, what the *implied* values of the outputs would have to be before it was justified to introduce a particular policy.

For example, taking screening for cervical cytology and simplifying somewhat, the level of risk varies for women of different age groups, social class and parity. It is thus possible to suggest, as

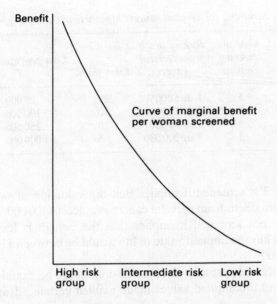

FIGURE 4.1 *Screening for cervical cancer, risk and benefit*

in Figure 4.1, that there is a continuous marginal benefit curve of screening which will fall as screening embraces women with smaller and smaller risks.

Let us assume for simplicity that the total costs per woman screened are constant (at say £5), that all positive cases would without intervention progress to death but with screening and treatment would be cured, and that the total costs of treatment arising from screening are equal to the total costs of treatment in the absence of screening. (These are obviously unrealistic assumptions; the complications of relaxing the assumptions are manageable but the simplicity of the assumptions helps understanding of the idea of implied values.) If there are, say, four identifiably different but numerically equal risk groups (of 1 million women each), and the risks are known, then a table on the following lines can be devised (Table 4.4). From this a 'cost per life saved' curve can be presented as in Figure 4.2.

Assuming that it is right to imply that a policy is only pursued if the benefits are thought to be at least as large as the costs, then if

TABLE 4.4   *Screening for cervical cancer: hypothetical costs per life saved*

Risk group	Cost of screening £million	Risk of death from cervical cancer	'Lives saved'	Cost per 'life saved' £
1	5	1 in 5 000	200	25 000
2	5	1 in 20 000	50	100 000
3	5	1 in 50 000	20	250 000
4	5	1 in 200 000	5	1 000 000

risk group 2 is screened it implies that the valuation of saving a woman from death from cervical cancer is at least £100 000. If risk group 3 is not screened it implies that the benefit is less than £250 000. Thus the implied value of life would be between £100 000 and £250 000.

If a number of past and current decisions could be examined in this way and the implied values made explicit certain advantages

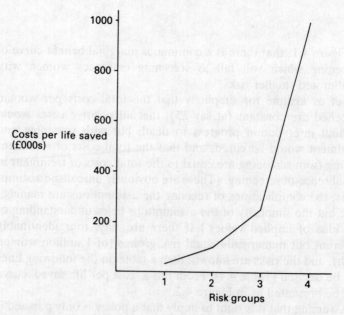

FIGURE 4.2   *Screening for cervical cancer: hypothetical costs per life saved*

would result. First, from past decisions it might be possible to establish a consistent set of implied values for various outputs which could perhaps then be used explicitly in future decisions. Second, if the values emerging for like outputs from past and current decisions are not consistent (as may well be the case) then immediately there is a case for examining why and attempting to ensure greater consistency in future. Third, the very process of examining implied values helps to increase awareness of the fact that value judgements are inherent in resource allocation decisions in health care.

Against such a background it can be seen that such studies and awareness will lead to improved decision-making for the future. Although these investigations fall short of an ideal application of cost–benefit analysis the use of the philosophy and framework of cost–benefit analysis can provide invaluable assistance in decision-making on resource allocation questions. (For a fuller discussion of these issues see Mooney [48]).

As well as the question of valuation of benefits, other issues are important in the application of cost–benefit analysis. For example, it has to be recognised that the benefits and costs are strictly speaking *social* benefits and social costs because cost–benefit analysis is concerned with social welfare as a whole. In other words no matter on whom the costs and benefits fall – the NHS, social work departments, individual patients, the community at large – they are relevant to the cost–benefit framework. The costs, as already indicated in the section on the approach to cost–effectiveness analysis, can often go far beyond financial costs. For example, if a daughter has to sacrifice employment or leisure opportunities to look after an ageing mother at home then these costs are relevant to cost–benefit analysis; the same applies to non-health benefits bestowed on individuals because of health-care policies. Although it will frequently be the case that not all costs and benefits can be measured and evaluated, none the less, in meeting the requirement that all costs and all benefits that arise from the project under consideration are at least identified, cost–benefit analysis performs a valuable role.

In terms of deciding *how much* of a particular service to supply the decision rule is to equate 'marginal social cost' with 'marginal social benefit'. This has already been touched on in chapter 3 in the context of deciding on the balance between different services or sub-programmes. Here the issue is considered in the context of deciding how much of one particular service to provide when there is no immediate budget constraint. This is shown diagrammatically in Figure 4.3.

The margin is the last unit of output. Thus the marginal social cost is the social cost of producing the last unit of output and the marginal social benefit is the social benefit provided by the last unit of output. If the level of output is below Q_1 (say Q_2) marginal benefit is greater than marginal cost and additional units could be provided which would yield additional positive net benefit and the area of net benefit VXW is being lost.

If the level of output is above Q_1 (say Q_3) marginal cost is greater than marginal benefit and there is a negative net marginal benefit. The point at which net benefit is maximised is thus where marginal cost equals marginal benefit, that is the level of output Q_1. Thus the marginal costs (and the marginal benefits) have a

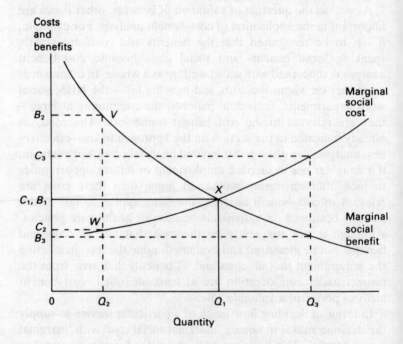

FIGURE 4.3   *Equating marginal costs and benefits*

particular significance in determining the right level of provision of a service.

What is contained within costs, marginal or otherwise, is partly dependent on the time scale. Some costs are fixed over a period of years, others are variable over a period of months or even weeks. Building costs are fixed over a number of years; some catering costs are variable from day to day. In deciding on the cost of a particular project it is therefore necessary to know the relevant time scale and the variability of costs over this period.

When costs are incurred is also relevant to their valuation and is related to the theory of discounting and present values. Even in real terms (that is omitting the question of inflation) the value of costs (and benefits) varies with time. There are a number of reasons for this. First, most of us are myopic and simply have a preference for goods and services now rather than later. Second, the future is uncertain (for example, we may not be alive). Third, if we receive £1 now and invest it, it will normally (assuming a positive real rate of interest) be worth more in a year's time. Fourth, because of economic growth the satisfaction obtained from an extra £1 of income is greater now than in the future (that is the marginal utility of income diminishes). For all these reasons there is a need to ensure that costs (and benefits) are considered at a particular point in time even although they may be spread over time. This is normally taken as the present time and hence 'present values' of costs and benefits are calculated. This is achieved by applying a discount rate to costs and benefits arising in the future. Fortunately (or perhaps unfortunately, since there is so much dispute about the calculations) the public sector discount rate has been determined by the Treasury and there is no need to calculate it for individual projects. Its current value is 5 per cent.

It is applied as follows. Assume the capital costs incurred in year 0 of a particular project are £500 000, that the running costs are £50 000 per annum, that the life of the project is 10 years and the scrap value at the end zero. Then although the total costs through time of the project are £1 million (£500 000 + 10 × £50 000) the present value of the costs (the relevant value) is derived as follows.

In year 0, the present time, the present value of the £500 000 capital costs is £500 000. In year 1, the £50 000 of running costs is to be valued at its present value which is given by the expression £50 000/1.05, where the discount rate is 5 per cent. This is equal to

£47 619. Another way to look at this is that if £47 619 were invested in year 0 at 5 per cent to meet the running costs in year 1, with interest it would amount to £50 000 (that is, £47 619 + 5 per cent of £47 619 = £50 000). Similar calculations would then be made to establish the present value of £50 000 running costs in year 2 that is £50 000/1.05^2; and so on.

The present value of the total costs of the project is

$$£500\,000 + \frac{£50\,000}{1.05} + \frac{£50\,000}{1.05^2} + \frac{£50\,000}{1.05^3} + \ldots + \frac{£50\,000}{1.05^{10}}$$

which equals £886 080.

The question of 'production functions' and the measurement of output is also a difficulty in cost–benefit studies. The nature of health care is such that often health care outputs are difficult to define, quantify and value. Frequently, although there is little doubt that a particular care regime provides an improvement in health, the quantification of such improvement is difficult. This is not an issue that economists can solve. It is one for the medical profession and here the growth in randomised controlled trials is valuable. It must be apparent that unless knowledge exists in some form about the effectiveness of a type of care, valuation of it, using cost–benefit analysis, is just not possible.

In some instances there may be certain risks associated with a project – it will become outdated, it will breakdown, etc. Again, some doubts may exist about just how effective a particular policy will be. In such instances different assumptions should be used to see how sensitive the results are to variations in the assumptions used. Such 'sensitivity analysis' is an important ingredient in cost–benefit studies when uncertainty or doubt exists about the size or value of the various parameters involved.

Cost–benefit analysis can thus be seen to be a valuable evaluative approach in health care. It is still at an early stage of development as a technique. But as a philosophy and a framework for consideration of policy options it can be of considerable assistance in decision-making. Whereas the issues of valuation of benefits must by and large remain the subjective province of the decision-makers, some progress can be made with existing valuation techniques and the use of implied values can at least engender a greater consistency in health policy-making. An understanding of cost–benefit analysis can also ensure that appropriate costs are identified and valued. While as yet (and perhaps for ever – which may be a good thing) cost–benefit analysis cannot act as a decision making tool in health care, its potential as a decision-aiding tool remains underexploited.

Conclusion

This chapter has outlined the nature of the techniques of cost–effectiveness analysis and cost–benefit analysis, the former being primarily concerned with the 'how' and the latter with the 'whether' and 'how much'. Clearly, as chapter 7 will demonstrate, problems do arise in the application of these techniques which cannot always be fully overcome – problems of data availability, cost and benefit measurement, lack of ideal output measures, and so on. None the less it is important that, if the use of these techniques is to grow in the health service and be seen to be useful, more and more health-service staff and decision-makers should be familiar with the theory and concepts underlying the techniques. Indeed it can be argued that the growth in the usage of the term 'cost–benefit' has been much more rapid that the growth of understanding of cost–benefit analysis. Unless this is corrected, and the situation is improving, there is a grave danger that the usefulness of cost–benefit analysis will not be fully appreciated.

But perhaps just as important as the techniques themselves is the very simple but important thinking underlying the approach of cost–benefit, that is, that we should only do those things where the benefits are greater than the costs and stop doing those things where this is not the case. The application of the techniques is not always easy; the understanding of the type of thinking involved is.

Williams [71] has pointed to the dangers that 'the weak-spirited ... (may) ... abandon the cost–benefit approach as too deman- ding, and return with relief to more comfortable ways.' But he continues:

The trouble with the more comfortable ways is that they foster the illusion that, if cost–benefit analysis is not done, the issues which it poses can be avoided, whereas the reality is that these issues are all still present, and they all still have to be resolved. If health-services planning is not to be based on the principles that unwitting decisions are likely to be better than witting decisions, then the cost–benefit approach must become a part of every decision-maker's intellectual equipment.

Many readers may well be directly concerned in decision-making about resource use in the health service. It is perhaps a fitting way to end a chapter concerned primarily with theory and concepts to provide some very practical guidance for those faced with such decisions. The following 'checklist' provided by Williams [71] is aimed at those faced with deciding on 'a studied recommendation about use of resources.'

1. What precisely is the question which the study was trying to answer?
2. What is the question that it has actually answered?
3. What are the assumed objectives of the activity studied?
4. By what measures are these represented?
5. How are they weighted?
6. Do they enable us to tell whether the objectives are being attained?
7. What range of options was considered?
8. What other options might there have been?
9. Were they rejected, or not considered, for good reasons?
10. Would their inclusion have been likely to change the results?
11. Is anyone likely to be affected who has not been considered in the analysis?
12. If so, why are they excluded?
13. Does the notion of cost go wider or deeper than the expenditure of the agency concerned?
14. If not, is it clear that these expenditures cover all the resources used and accurately represent their value if released for other uses?
15. If so, is the line drawn so as to include all potential beneficiaries and losers, and are resources costed at their value in their best alternative use?
16. Is the differential timing of the items in the streams of benefits and costs suitably taken care of (e.g. by discounting and, if so, at what rate)?

17. Where there is uncertainty, or there are known margins of error, is it made clear how sensitive the outcome is to these elements?
18. Are the results, on balance, good enough for the job in hand?
19. Has anyone else done better?

Appendix

An example of a proposed health indicator

Culyer, Lavers and Williams [9] suggest that 'to generate a state-of-health indicator which will also serve as an effectiveness measure, it will be necessary to devise an algorithm which will encompass both (a) medical data and judgments and (b) social judgments, with each expressed numerically in a standardised manner, yet clearly distinguished one from another'.

Both intensity and duration need to be measured but for the purposes of exposition Culyer *et al.* restrict their attention to intensity which they identify as having two dimensions – pain and restriction of activity. The initial stage in establishing indicators is to describe particular conditions in terms of these two dimensions. This is shown in Figure A4.1. α, β, γ and δ relate to degrees of painfulness (for example, mildly uncomfortable). a, b, c, d and e describe restriction of activity (for example, confined to house). O, × and Δ each refers to different medical conditions or combinations thereof. Thus in Figure A4.1 it is assumed that the consensus of medical observers is that the medical condition Δ has a painfulness level of γ and a level of e for the degree of restriction. For the medical condition O the consensus is β, c and for × it is δ, e. (If no consensus exists for a particular condition further study may be required to specify it more precisely.) Assuming each condition can be specified in terms of painfulness and restriction, the next step is to establish the relative intensity of each state (for example is the combination γ, a better or worse than the combination β, c?). As Culyer *et al.* emphasise, this type of comparison 'is essentially a *social* judgment ... but may have to be made in practice by medical people'. This step is shown in Figure A4.2.

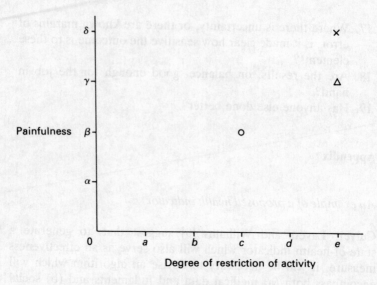

FIGURE A4.1 *Medical conditions classified by painfulness and degree of restriction*

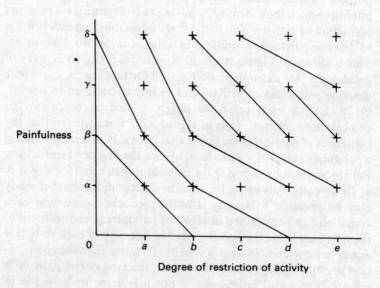

FIGURE A4.2 *Contour lines of combinations of pain and restriction*

Each combination of pain category and restriction category is compared. Those that are viewed as about the same (in terms of the social humanitarian benefit of avoiding them) are linked by 'contour' lines, as depicted in Figure A4.2. In the example shown, the combinations $(\beta, 0)$; (α, a); and $(0, b)$ are equivalent to each other, but better than $(\delta, 0)$; (β, a); (α, b); and $(0, d)$. Thus the further is the contour from the origin $(0, 0)$ the worse is the set of conditions lying on the contour.

This stage of the generation of indicators would thus provide ordinal measures of health states. The next stage would be to move to cardinal measures and construct a points scale of intensity of ill-health. One scale suggested by Cuyler *et al.* is as follows:

> 0 = normal
> 1 = able to carry out normal activities, but with some pain or discomfort
> 2 = restricted to light activities only, but with little pain or discomfort
> 3–7 = various intermediate categories reflecting various degrees of pain and/or restriction of activity
> 8 = conscious, but in great pain and activity severely restricted
> 9 = unconscious
> 10 = dead

These numbers would be used as *weights* and not simply *rankings*. Thus society's judgements about the numbers would reflect the relative importance it attached to avoiding the different states; for example, state 6 is six times as bad as state 1 and three times as bad as state 2. Clearly judgements about such weights are not technical statements about health conditions but rather judgements related to *health policy*.

5
A Case Study in Programme Budgeting

As was indicated in chapter 2, the essence of programme budgeting in the health service is to provide a framework for planning health care.

It is all too easy for a health board or authority to become heavily engaged in *ad hoc* decisions on minor changes in resource allocation, in patching up deficiencies in individual services and in considering only the 3 per cent or so (and less in future) of development monies available each year. Programme budgeting does not eliminate the need to consider such questions – it provides a broader view of the service within which such questions can be considered in a more rational and informed way. It is, as Pole [52] states, 'a set of accounts which one hopes may be suggestive in itself and a basis for further analysis'.

For example, when a post of, say, a consultant paediatrician falls vacant it is unusual for a health authority to question whether or not it should be refilled. Even if the question is asked, it is usually extremely difficult for the authority to weigh up the implications of the choice and the simplest answer is to maintain the *status quo*. However, the authority may have previously decided to give increased priority to care of the elderly and mentally ill – if it has done so with the aid of programme budgeting it is better placed to see the effects and assess the merits of the appointment compared with other uses of the money because it can see the impact on the relativities of the resource use by various programmes. It may also be part of the policy of the authority to shift the emphasis of care towards the community services; a programme-budgeting framework will highlight this balance both within child care and for all programmes and may prompt the authority to question whether, even if the current balance between programmes is broadly correct, it would be more in line with its policy to shift the resources to community aspects of child care.

The case study described in this chapter was undertaken by the authors and others in the early 1970s as part of the Health Services Economics Project, financed by the Scottish Home and Health Department. (For an example of programme budgeting at national level see the DHSS priorities document [15]).

Methodology

In exploring the development of programme budgeting for use in the Grampian health area, which encompasses the north-east of Scotland, the researchers in the Health Services Economics Project team decided that the data to be used should be those readily available to all health boards from normal costing and activity returns and that no special surveys should be conducted. Because of this, certain assumptions had to be made to apportion various costs to the different programmes. Thus some accuracy was lost as compared with a system which used special surveys to obtain data in a more appropriate form than that which routinely existed. None the less the authors believe that the method used provides sufficiently accurate results for the purpose of strategic planning. Although the health service accounting systems differ in other parts of the United Kingdom, the principles involved in the methodology are applicable in all four services.

Programme structure

The programme headings used were as follows:

Medicine	Dental
Surgery	Ophthalmic
Elderly	Maternity
Mental	Child

The chosen structure of the programmes was such that in the hospital sector most individual specialties could be clearly identified with, and therefore their costs allocated to, programmes. This was true of both in-patient and out-patient services. Some specialties were less clearly allied with one particular programme and the choice of allocation of these depended on the use expected to be made of the programme budgets. For example, paediatric surgery could have been allocated to the child programme or the surgery programme; because of the organisation of the local service it was judged more relevant to allocate it to the former.

Of the primary care services, the General Medical and the General Pharmaceutical Services were allocated to medicine, the General Dental Service to dental and the General Ophthalmic Services to ophthalmology. In the community, health visiting and home nursing of the elderly were included in the elderly programme whereas visiting to children was included in the child programme, as were care of mothers and young children and the school health services. Domiciliary midwifery and health visiting associated with pregnancy were allocated to maternity. Expenditure on vaccination and immunisation was included in medicine. Mental health services in the community were allocated to the mental

Programme costs

The derivation of some of the costs needs explanation. One of the main difficulties in costing in-patient care is that without going to individual patient records it is not possible, and even then no easy task, to provide wholly accurate data about the use of services by specialty. In single-specialty hospitals the whole costs can be allocated directly to programmes but approximations have to be made in hospitals with more than one specialty. In this study the allocation method was as follows.

Hospital in-patients   In single-programme hospitals (for example, geriatric hospitals) the total costs were allocated directly to programmes. These costs amounted to over a third of total in-patient expenditure.

In joint-programme hospitals three types of costs were identified and treated in different ways.

(1) Ward costs (for example, for nursing and junior medical staff) for single-programme *wards* were allocated to the appropriate programmes. Ward costs for joint-programme wards were allocated to programmes in the same proportion as occupied beds in the different programmes in each of the wards concerned. Together they accounted for approximately 25 per cent of total in-patient expenditure.

(2) Certain other costs were allocated directly to programmes. They included cardiology (to medicine), radiotherapy (to surgery), surgical appliances and theatre (to surgery, except where there was identification with other programmes such as maternity and child) and electroencephalography (split equally between medicine and surgery). In total these were about 3 per cent of the total in-patient expenditure.

(3) All other costs (catering, heating and lighting, pharmacy, etc.) were allocated pro-rata with occupied bed days in each hospital and accounted for less than 40 per cent of in-patient expenditure remaining to be allocated. Although there is unlikely to be much loss of accuracy in allocating this group of items on this basis, clearly for some of the items allocated in this way – particularly pharmacy, physiotherapy, X-ray, transport and equipment – there must be some reservations about this method of allocation. However, this last group of items in multi-programme hospitals represented only 5 per cent of total in-patient expenditure, a percentage which did not, certainly initially, justify a special survey to find a more precise method of apportionment.

Hospital out-patients Hospital out-patients can be classified into two broad categories – specialty (for example general surgery and dermatology) and service (for example physiotherapy and X-ray). The allocation of out-patient costs was made on a similar basis to that adopted for in-patients except that *specialty* clinic sessions were used in place of occupied bed days. This assumes not only that specialty out-patient costs in a particular hospital can be attributed pro-rata with the number of specialty clinic sessions but also that service out-patient costs can also be attributed pro-rata with the number of specialty clinic sessions. These assumptions are a little crude and consequently out-patient costing for the programme budgets is an area where refinement of the procedure used is desirable.

Specialists   For specialists the total cost for each grade of specialists was divided by the number of whole time equivalent (WTE) specialists in that grade, to give an average cost per WTE specialist in that grade. Thereafter costs were allocated according to the number of WTE specialists in each grade in each specialty and thereby to programmes.

Community costs   For many items of community expenditure it was possible to allocate costs directly from the accounts. For others apportionment was required. For example, in health visiting and district nursing it was assumed that the cost of a visit was constant no matter to whom it was made. Primary care services were allocated directly to programmes from the accounts. Clearly the usefulness of this allocation for some policy questions is doubtful, particularly the decision to allocate all the costs of the General Medical and Pharmaceutical Services to the medicine programme, although, of course, the primary care components of the medicine programme can still be separately identified. None the less further refinement based on additional data is desirable.

Thus, some of the assumptions used in apportioning expenditure to the programmes can be questioned. However, given the decision to start with only data currently available to all health boards, such assumptions appear reasonable. Clearly there is a case for refining the data base by introducing a new coding system or for instituting small sample surveys to obtain more accurate methods of apportioning costs.

However, when the purpose of programme budgeting and the nature of the decisions likely to be taken in policy-making are remembered, the degree of accuracy in this study appears to be sufficient. To illustrate this, a few of the findings from analysis of the programme data are presented below.

Some findings

Figure 5.1 indicates how allocated expenditure (which is about 92 per cent of the total, most of the unallocated expenditure being on

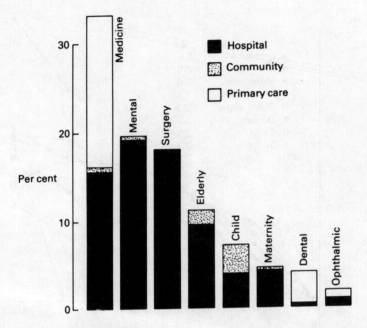

FIGURE 5.1   *Grampian AHB programme budgets, 1975/6: percentage of allocated expenditure by programme*

administration) was deployed across the eight different programmes in the Grampian Health Board's services for the year 1975/6. It should be noted that only current expenditure data are presented. The problems associated with valuation of capital are considerable and this is the main reason why it has been omitted.

The medicine programme is artificially high in that it contains all the costs of the General Medical and the General Pharmaceutical Services. Excluding these components, it is apparent that there are three very large, and very largely hospital-dominated, programmes – medicine, surgery and mental. The other five together account for less than 30 per cent of total expenditure in Grampian in 1975/6.

In Figure 5.2 the trends in expenditure through the six years 1970/1 to 1975/6 are presented. These are all at 1970/1 prices. Some of the growth patterns in Figure 5.2 are of interest. The most

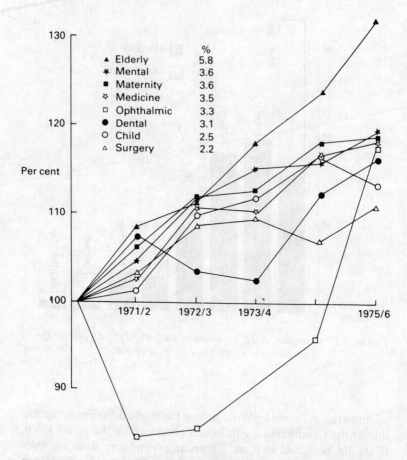

FIGURE 5.2 *Grampian AHB programme budgets: changes in expenditure (1970/1 prices) by programme 1970/1 to 1975/6 (expenditure in 1970/1 equals 100 for each programme)*

notable feature is the very similar total percentage growth of the programmes over this period. There is a suggestion here either that the health board (and its predecessor, the North East Regional Hospital Board) felt that the shares of most programmes in 1970/1 were about right and should be maintained or that the programmes have simply grown in what might be described as a disjointed incrementalist way. The main exception to this is the elderly programme which has grown at a noticeably higher rate than the other programmes. The somewhat strange growth path of the ophthalmic programme is largely a result of netting-out patient charges, which altered over this period.

Whether these growth patterns coincide with what was intended is not clear. However, the Grampian Health Board and its predecessor had over this period earmarked development funds for the elderly and mental programmes in equal absolute amounts because they wished them to have equal priority for development. The main reason why the elderly programme has grown faster is simply that it is a smaller programme than the mental. It could be argued that had the programme budgeting data been available earlier the earmarking of development monies might have been made not on the basis of equal absolute amounts but in proportion to the size of the respective programmes, thus maintaining equal priority. This provides a simple example of how programme budgeting data, had they been available at the time, might have influenced one particular decision.

Of course, the intermediate outputs from these programmes changed through time as well. For the in-patient programmes, this is shown (in Figure 5.3) by bringing together changes in expenditure (at 1970/1 prices), bed days and discharges. Taking 1970/1 as 100, Figure 5.3 indicates the level of these three factors in 1975/6 for each of the eight programmes.

It is clear from Figure 5.3 that while all programmes increased their total expenditure (by 30 per cent in the elderly to less than 10 per cent in dental) discharges fell in two cases (child and maternity) and bed utilisation fell in all except ophthalmic. Maternity is particularly noteworthy in that, while expenditure rose in real terms by 20 per cent, bed utilisation fell by 22 per cent and discharges by over 11 per cent. In effect this was a rise in unit cost per bed day occupied of 53 per cent and per discharge of 34 per cent, equivalent to average annual growth rates over the 5-year period of over 9 per cent and 6 per cent respectively. The next highest rises were per bed day in the elderly (35 per cent) and per discharge in the child programme (25 per cent). It is also worthy of note that if the elderly programme is excluded (because of special treatment over the period) and the two programmes with the smallest hospital component, ophthalmic and dental, are also excluded the five remaining programmes – child, mental, medi-

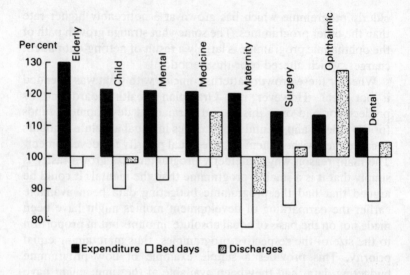

■ Expenditure □ Bed days ▨ Discharges

FIGURE 5.3   *Grampian AHB programme budgets–in-patient programmes: percentage changes in expenditure (1970/1 prices), bed utilisation and discharges by programme, 1975/6 compared with 1970/1 (discharges not presented for long-stay programmes)*

cine, maternity and surgery – all grew in expenditure terms by very similar proportions (between 14 and 22 per cent) despite very different growth patterns in bed utilisation and discharges. Thus discharges in medicine increased by 12 per cent while those in maternity fell by 11 per cent, despite almost identical proportional increases in expenditure. Again the fall in the use of beds in the mental programme was only 7 per cent, that in maternity was over 22 per cent yet both programmes expanded in expenditure terms by about 20 per cent.

Similar analyses can be presented for the out-patient sector and for the bulk of the community services (in terms of visits). It is more difficult in the primary care services, for some of which activity data are lacking. None the less for all the programmes, as has been shown, trends in total expenditure can be described through time and within most sectors these expenditure data can be set against activity data as a proxy for output.

A word of caution is, however, required. It is not the intention of programme budgeting to present a case for cutting maternity care or increasing care of the mentally ill. As Pole [52] indicates 'the programme budget is basically only an account of expenditure, analysed by output-orientated categories. In some cases the mere revelation of the order of magnitude of expenditure on various programmes may by itself give clear indications of priorities for expenditure, but it cannot be relied upon to do so.' The budgets can provide only a framework within which a health board or authority can make an overview of its policy over the recent past and begin to ask questions about those trends which give rise to some element of surprise or potential imbalance, such as where the board or authority sees a particular trend as unexpected or unintentional. In this way the programme budgets provide a mechanism for selection in deciding which programmes merit more detailed appraisal and investigation. For example, it might be that the Grampian Health Board had fully intended that the quality of maternity care should rise substantially and to this end were content to see significantly increased expenditure going to this programme in terms of the costs per bed day and per discharge. But if this is not so then in consultation with the appropriate groups it might wish to determine whether or not the apparent priority being given to maternity is justified in terms of some increase in the quality of care in this programme.

The approach of programme budgeting was also used as a framework for consideration of the proposals in *The Way Ahead* [59] the Scottish White Paper on priorities in health care (comparable to the English document *Priorities for Health and Social Services* [15]). This document embraced several principles such as 'lessening the growth rate of the acute sector of the hospital service in order to finance essential development in other sectors' and 'continued improvements in hospital and community health services for the elderly, the mentally ill and the mentally handicapped'. At the same time *The Way Ahead* forecast an overall growth in expenditure of 10 per cent up to 1981/2.

At this point it is necessary to bring in important health-care considerations for the future, for example, changes in the technology of care. Presented below are rather crude expenditure scenarios which clearly need to be viewed against expected changes in, say, demands for different types of health care or technological change. However, allowing for expected changes in the relevant populations, if the growth rates on a *per capita* basis for the individual programmes had been linearly extrapolated to 1981/2 and the relevant expected populations at that time applied to these figures, the growth in expenditure required to meet this would have been 23 per cent. There was, therefore, no prospect of continuing to expand the services as rapidly as had been the case in the past – a phenomenon already recognised but not previously quantified in this way.

As a first crude expenditure scenario for 1981/2, the individual programmes' extrapolated growth rates were all scaled down by 10/23 to accommodate them within the anticipated overall growth rate of 10 per cent. The scenario for the Grampian Health Board in 1981 was then as shown in Table 5.1. This crude scenario suggested that the Grampian Health Board was already reflecting some of the priorities outlined in *The Way Ahead*. For example, there was a fall in the share of expenditure on surgery and increase in both mental and the elderly. Other scenarios which might more firmly endorse the recommendations of *The Way Ahead* could have been devised, but at least as important was the need to link the programme budgeting information to forecasts of changes in demand and the nature of care regimes over the coming years so that the effects of a range of priorities and policies could be forecast.

Programme budgeting within a programme

Programme budgeting can of course provide a similar framework for planning within individual programmes. Without going into details, Figure 5.4 provides relevant data from a study by Gray and Steele [32] on the sub-programme budgets of antenatal, labour/birth and postnatal in maternity care.

The use of programme budgeting has been growing in recent years. The Department of Health and Social Security in London has used it as the basis for its planning [15] and both the DHSS in Belfast and SHHD in Edinburgh have used it to monitor activities and plans. For example, in SHAPE it is reported that despite the priorities laid down in the earlier priorities document for Scotland (*The Way Ahead*), programme budgeting showed that trends in expenditure were not in line with stated priorities. In its pursuit of 'Health for All in the Year 2000' WHO has enlisted the help of

TABLE 5.1 *Scenario for 1981, if extrapolated growth rates are all scaled down by a factor of 10/23 (1975/6 prices, £000's)*

	Medicine	Mental	Surgery	Elderly	Child	Maternity	Dental	Ophthalmic	Total
1975/6	13 742 (33.4)	7 949 (19.3)	7 439 (18.1)	4 634 (11.3)	2 972 (7.2)	1 896 (4.6)	1 675 (4.1)	785 (1.9)	41 091 (100.0)
1981/2	15 254 (33.8)	8 823 (19.6)	7 922 (17.6)	5 190 (11.5)	3 180 (7.1)	2 029 (4.5)	1 826 (4.0)	871 (1.9)	45 095 (100.0)
Percentage growth	11	11	6.5	12	7	7	9	11	10

Figures in brackets show the percentage shares of total allocated expenditure

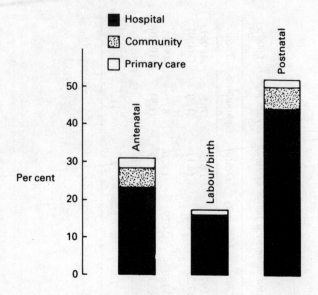

FIGURE 5.4   *Grampian maternity sub-programme budgets, 1976/7*

programme budgeting. Yet its use remains less than optimal. It can be an inexpensive way of getting a greater benefit from health care planning.

Similar types of 'sub-programme budgets' could be devised for other programmes. The important aspects to note are that again the sub-programmes are 'output-orientated' and that it is potentially easier to see and compare the nature of the outputs of sub-programmes which have a common target population.

Conclusion

A method has been devised of allocating costs of care to programmes to create a programme budgeting framework for policy-making. Because it is based on currently available data it is relatively cheap to produce and, although some further accuracy might be desired, the information has been shown to reflect what is happening sufficiently to have already proved useful to the Grampian Health Board in planning and monitoring its policy choices. It can be used for highlighting options both within and between programmes of care. Although it does not appraise or evaluate options it does help to focus on where to apply techniques of evaluation while still creating a comprehensive view of the services provided by a health board or authority.

6

Marginal Analysis: a Case Study in Care of the Elderly

In chapter 3 the approach and purpose of marginal analysis were described. It is a framework that allows identification of those parts of services which are most likely to be affected by an increase or decrease in resources. It thus allows planners to make more appropriate comparisons of costs, potential benefits and opportunity costs of alternative allocations or shifts in resources than they would make by looking at total or average costs and benefits. The underlying philosophy is that for operational plans it is only necessary to look at these marginal costs and benefits because, given limited health-care resources, only small shifts in allocation are possible before techniques, values and therefore benefits from particular resources have changed.

To test whether it was possible to apply marginal analysis not just as a philosophy in asking questions but as a technique for planning, a study was mounted into balance of long-term care for the elderly in Aberdeen. (Some aspects of this have been previously described by one of the authors [47].) The hypotheses to be tested were

(1) that those who provide care can and do rank, even if not consciously, the degree of urgency or priority of the competing claims for their services and thereby can pick out those groups with the greatest priority for a change of location;
(2) that the pertinent groups can be described in terms which allow comparison of the implied relative benefits from making

a shift of resources between services or from an increase or decrease in overall resources;

(3) that the relevant costs for these groups can be calculated.

The particular field for study was chosen because the Grampian Health Board's Care of the Elderly Programme Committee had identified an imbalance between services for support at home or in sheltered housing, in residential homes and in hospital as the main factor which it wished to see corrected. Thus, the ultimate purpose of the study was to devise a relatively quick and reliable way of (a) describing the level of dependence, (b) calculating the costs of caring for those groups of elderly who might be affected by a shift of resources from one facility to another or an overall increase or decrease in resources and (c) thereby on the basis of such information to improve the balance between them. While the choice to be made might be a 'one-off' shift in resources because of the time required to carry out a transfer of staff or buildings, it was also hoped that the technique would allow monitoring of time-trends in the nature of the dependence of marginal clients and in the costs of care to see whether intended change was actually occurring. The results presented here relate only to the one-off analysis.

Method

The survey

Random selections of district nurses and of health visitors and all the matrons of local authority residential homes for the elderly in Aberdeen were asked to participate in the study. There were three main reasons for basing the study on these groups of staff: first, one of the aims was to keep the costs of obtaining the necessary information within reasonable bounds and effort. The survey of the elderly in the community (that is, not in an institution) was thus conducted during routine visits by health visitors and district nurses. In the residential homes each matron completed a questionnaire for each of the residents of her own home. Second, the nurses and the matrons have the advantage of being familiar with the elderly they are caring for and they are often instrumental in seeking movements of their clients or patients. Third, over 90 per cent of those on the waiting list for residential homes and the majority who are assessed at home for long-stay geriatric or psychogeriatric care are being visited by either a district nurse or a health visitor. Thus the great majority of potentially 'marginal' community clients will be picked up during routine visiting of the elderly by the health visitors and district nurses.

The survey of the elderly in the community was conducted at the beginning of June 1976. A random sample of 35 district nurses was asked to complete questionnaires for the first 20 elderly clients visited by each nurse after 9 a.m. on Monday 31 May. At the same time a random sample of 50 health visitors each completed a similar survey for 10 elderly clients. From these samples, data were obtained on 659 elderly people being visited by district nurses (there were 41 duplicate questionnaires in the 700) and on 500 elderly people being visited by health visitors. Using data on the frequency of visiting the sample was weighted to give pictures of all the elderly being visited by district nurses and by health visitors.

In addition each nurse or health visitor completed a second questionnaire in which she was asked to indicate which of the clients for whom she had completed questionnaires she would, assuming places were available, recommend for (a) sheltered housing; (b) residential home and (c) long-stay hospital. These in effect are the 'marginal' clients as judged by the staff caring for them.

In the residential homes all the matrons completed questionnaires for each of the residents of their own homes – a total of 366. Again those clients who were 'marginal' were identified, both at the low dependency level (that is, those who might be recommended for a move to the community) and at the high dependency level (that is those who might be recommended for long-stay hospitals). These margins were split in two ways by asking about recommended moves with no change in the number of places in the homes and then with a reduction in places in the homes.

It should be noted that it was not so much the *numbers* of individuals placed on the margins which was being sought out but, rather, a description of their *characteristics* first to see whether their dependence, as a group, differed from that of other groups and second to allow decision-makers to see who would be affected by different shifts in the balance of care, for example, the type of people who would move to residential home if more places were available. Because of the small numbers of elderly people in the sample who lived in sheltered housing, they are not reported on separately.

Descriptive data

The first, descriptive questionnaire for all the elderly included questions about characteristics used routinely by staff to describe levels of disability and dependence on others in respect of mobility, personal care (including incontinence), companionship and living conditions. The questions were not intended to identify finely scaleable degrees of dependence but, where relevant, the broad categorisation of 'able alone', 'able with help' and 'not able' was used. Additional characteristics used by staff as indicative of high risk of need for support were included, for example, 'all members of household aged 75 or more'. Questions were also included about use of services and these were used to assist in deriving cost data.

The way in which disability and dependence were used in the study requires comment. The care of the Elderly Programme Committee had defined their long-term goal as 'reduction of dependence on others – family, friends or services'. Their short-term goal was to try to meet, with the most appropriate service, the dependence already existing in the elderly in Grampian. Thus, benefit would be obtained if more dependence were met and efficiency would be increased if the benefits of meeting different types of dependence arose by improving the match of the various services to these types of dependence.

In the study reported here it would have been possible to address any one of the three issues: (i) redeployment of existing resources; (ii) deployment of additional resources; and (iii) which facility to cut if resources were decreased for the programme as a whole. As will be seen below, we have chosen to report on (ii) although the data collected would have allowed us to consider the other two issues as well.

A secondary purpose of the study was to test which characteristics out of a wide range would be most useful for picking up changes over time and which characteristics could be discarded in any subsequent use of the method.

Disability was included in the descriptive characteristics to see whether and how the *nature* and prevalence of the characteristics of the marginal populations varied with different types of dependence. For example, it could reasonably be expected that physical disability would be more likely to appear as a distinguishing variable on the margin for geriatric care than on the margin for psychogeriatric hospital care.

Costing

The purpose of estimating costs was to be able to indicate the costs involved in different locations for the relevant groups. It should be noted that it is not just the costs involved for the health service and social work services which are relevant. For example, the costs falling on the elderly themselves of living in the community are relevant costs and estimates were made of these. In addition it must be emphasised that no estimate has been included of the costs falling on relatives and friends involved in caring for the elderly. The reason for this is simply because of the difficulties involved in first obtaining the necessary data (on employment, leisure and even perhaps marital opportunities forgone) and second placing monetary values on these costs. The fact that these costs have had to be omitted is particularly unfortunate because all too often health service decision-makers not only omit such considerations but at times appear even to deny their relevance. Others have experienced difficulties here. For example, Wright and his colleagues [76] did not estimate these costs 'because our research sponsors requested us not to do so'. (This is particularly unfortunate as the sponsors in this instance were DHSS!)

Community population costs   For community populations, unit cost data for visits by domiciliary support services were estimated and multiplied by the frequency of visiting recorded in the study to give an annual cost of such services (see Table 6.4). It should be noted that the time of voluntary workers (for example, church visitors) was not included although clearly there may be a positive opportunity cost involved (for example they might have been doing other voluntary work). Living costs for the elderly in the community were based on the Family Expenditure Survey [12] (FES) for 1975 (see Table 6.5). Housing costs were treated separately because the housing expenditure in the FES is not a true reflection of the resource costs involved. For housing costs rateable values were obtained and very approximate costs were estimated on the basis of these. Two different assumptions were used for individuals not living alone: (i) there is a zero opportunity cost attached to the space vacated if an individual moves to an institution and (ii) there is a positive opportunity cost which is a function of the difference in value of the property occupied by one and two person households.

Residential home population costs   The annual equivalent of the capital cost per place was estimated by assuming a life of 60 years and discounting at 10 per cent, the public sector discount rate at that time. For running costs, only caring staff time was assumed to vary with dependence and the allocation of these costs to the individuals in the different populations was based on information obtained in interviews with matrons. Caring costs were allocated in the ratio 70:23:20 according to whether the resident was placed on the hospital margin, no margin or the community margin respectively (see Table 6.6). The extent of visiting to the homes by support services was small and appeared not to depend on whether an individual was on a margin or not. They were therefore assumed equal for all residents (see Table 6.6). The total costs were then obtained by adding capital costs, 'non-caring' costs, caring costs and support service costs (see Table 6.6).

Hospital costs   The capital cost per annum per place for a 60-bed geriatric long-stay unit in Aberdeen was estimated (assuming a discount rate of 10 per cent and a 60 year life). Using nursing dependency data and assuming that caring staff comprise 35 per cent of running costs, the range of running costs was then estimated and added to the capital costs. These costs are rather tentative because, as should be noted, no special survey was undertaken in the hospitals and the hospital costs are based solely on geriatric costs and therefore exclude psychogeriatric costs which could not be identified separately.

Identification of people who might move

The second questionnaire has been mentioned already but deserves further explanation of its purpose. The conditions under which the staff were asked to recommend someone for a move were those of variations in availability of resources, either in the present location of the elderly person or in an alternative. It was fully explained to the staff that the survey was intended to describe what the actual thresholds were for various facilities and what degrees of dependence and costs of care characterise those people who were likely to be affected by a shift, increase or decrease of resources. It was also made clear that no *individual* would be directly affected by the judgement of the member of staff.

Thus marginal analysis shifts the focus to highlight what is actually happening (often despite contradictory policies at a higher level) and away from the more usual approach of assessing the size of the gap between 'met' and 'unmet' need without reference to the level of resources likely to be available.

Results

Only a summary of the findings of the study is given here. A description of the total case-loads of district nurses and health visitors has been published elsewhere and detailed tables of the descriptions of the populations and the costs of their care are available from the authors.

The identification of marginal population

The distribution of the study population is shown in Table 6.1.

The marginal populations were compared with the non-marginal populations, and with one another, for the prevalence of disability and dependence factors. The comparisons were first made by a straightforward examination of individual characteristics within the various groups; second, to enable the variation in several factors to be examined simultaneously, the technique of discriminant function analysis was used. By this means it was also possible

TABLE 6.1   *Numbers of clients placed on margins, by type of staff*

	Margin			
Staff	Community	Sheltered housing	Residential home	Hospital	Total number in sample
District nurses	—	93	81	38	659
Health visitors	—	140	101	42	500
Matrons*	14	28	—	68	366

* The numbers placed on the margin given a reduction in the number of residential home places. (The numbers placed on the margin given the existing number of residential home places were: 3, 15 and 44.)

to identify the particular variables within a set which contributed most to differentiation of the groups.

People in the community Although the two services (health vistors and district nurses) had dissimilar types of case load they identified similar margins. Differences, significant at the 1 per cent level, were found in most characteristics between each of their marginal and non-marginal groups with the discrimination greatest for the hospital margin and least for that of sheltered housing.

It was possible to achieve significant discrimination for the hospital margin by the simultaneous examination of factors of continence, ability for personal care, mental impairment and self-neglect. One discriminant function, based on suitable weighting of these and other less important parameters, classified correctly 89.0 per cent of the grouped cases. For the residential home margin, living alone, locomotor difficulties under present living conditions and general problems with mobility had the greatest discriminating powers. Again suitable weighting of these and other less important factors enabled significant discrimination to be made, with 78.9 per cent correct classifications.

People in residential homes There were differences between the marginal and total populations for all the disability and dependency factors. The discrimination was greatest for the hospital (geriatric) margin, but mobility had high discriminating powers for both hospital and community margins.

Comparison of characteristics of marginal populations

The second hypothesis being tested was that marginal populations could be described in terms which allowed comparison of the implied benefits from making a shift of resources to or between services. The prevalence of the factors used in the study to reflect disability and dependence were compared between the various populations in the community and in residential homes (by definition, the environmental factors were not comparable). The similarity between the profiles of those on the hospital margins was very marked in several particulars, although in general those on the residential homes hospital margin were more likely to be severely afflicted than were those from the community (see Table 6.2).

Interestingly, the residential home margin in the community had a strong resemblance to the main group of people in residential homes whereas the community margin in the residential homes resembled the non-marginal group in the community (see Table 6.3).

TABLE 6.2   *Hospital margins: percentage of population with listed characteristics*

	Hospital margins		Not on hospital margin	
	Community popn* (38)	Residential homes popn (68)	Community popn* (621)	Residential homes popn (298)
Frequent falls	54.1	70.6	18.2	28.9
Night confusion	48.8	61.8	9.5	15.1
Locomotor difficulties	50.0	73.5	22.9	40.9
Mental impairment	65.8	79.4	17.8	42.6
Unable alone:				
self care	89.5	94.1	43.3	69.1
mobility – bed	78.9	73.5	35.4	33.6
mobility – house	78.9	70.6	37.4	33.2
mobility – stairs	87.9	88.2	56.4	57.0
mobility – outside	90.0	89.7	65.1	61.3

* District nurses' sample

TABLE 6.3   *Residential home and community margins: percentage of population with listed characteristics*

Factor	Community popn† (372)	Res. home popn on community margin (42)	Community popn* on res. home margin (101)	Res. home popn≠ (256)
Frequent falls	13.3	14.3	36.4	31.3
Locomotor difficulties	21.3	16.7	49.5	44.9
Mental impairment	11.1	9.5	44.6	48.0
Night confusion	2.0	2.4	18.1	17.2

* Health visitors' sample
† Residential home and hospital margins excluded
≠Hospital and community margins excluded

Thus it would appear that the matrons in charge of the residential homes, the health visitors and the district nurses had similar, identifiable notions of community, residential home and hospital clients. The chosen factors were ones in common use by the staff involved in the survey. They were not intended to reflect fine degrees of difference in dependence; indeed, the search for such accuracy has consumed the efforts of many researchers in the past two decades and many difficulties still remain (see, for example, Wright [75]). Some further refinement could have been sought but, since the purpose of the study was an initial exploration of the feasibility of applying marginal analysis, the cost of greater detail was not considered to be justified until the general feasibility was proven. Despite this, the differences which emerged between margins in the prevalences of the dependency factors accord with the views of all the staff concerned and of the Care of the Elderly Programme Committee.

Costs

For the community populations only the results for the health visitor population are presented in this section. (Those for the

TABLE 6.4   *Annual costs* per capita *of support services for health visitor populations*

	Population		
	Not on margin £	On residential home margin £	On hospital margin £
District nurse	15	31	74
Health visitor	7	11	12
GP	32	47	102
Home help	74	164	140
Meals on wheels	1	10	3
Physiotherapist	0	0	0
Chiropodist	1	1	2
Social worker	0	7	2
Total	**131**	**272**	**334**

district nurse population are available on request from the authors.)

What is of particular interest for marginal analysis, as Table 6.4 shows, is that proceeding across the four populations listed, from the non-marginal population through to the hospital marginal population, the costs tend to increase. (This was also true of the district nurse population.)

These costs, together with living costs and housing costs (using assumptions (i) and (ii) on p. 83), are presented in Table 6.5 to give the total costs per annum per elderly client in the different populations in the community. The differences emerging in the housing costs, and indeed in the total costs, for the three populations considered are very much a function of the proportion of single-person households in the populations. Hence the assumption used for the cost of space occupied by an individual in a multi-person household is of no little importance.

The various costs in the residential homes for the three populations are shown in Table 6.6. Given the evidence from the survey and the assumptions used the differences between the total costs per resident per annum in the three populations is solely a function of variation in the caring staff costs.

TABLE 6.5   *Annual costs* per capita *for health visitor populations*

	Population			
	Not on margin	*On sheltered housing margin*	*On residential home margin*	*On hospital margin*
Services	122	171	272	335
Housing (i)	406	516	746	403
(ii)	572	652	817	570
Living	750	750	750	750
Total (i)	**1 278**	**1 437**	**1 768**	**1 488**
(ii)	**1 444**	**1 573**	**1 839**	**1 655**

In the hospitals, the estimated annual cost of the least dependent was £5900 per patient (£900 for capital and £5000 for running costs) compared with an overall average cost of £7200 and for the most dependent £7400.

The estimated annual cost figures for the different populations in the three locations of community, residential home and hospital are brought together in Table 6.7. Presented with these are the estimated annual cost figures for an average elderly person in the health visitor population in the community, in a residential home and in hospital.

In examining these cost estimates for the different populations two points must be made. First, the estimates of costs were not as

TABLE 6.6   *Annual costs per resident, by population*

	Population		
	On community margin £	*Not on margin* £	*On hospital margin* £
Caring staff	430	490	1 500
Other running	1 150	1 150	1 150
Capital	900	900	900
Support services	70	70	70
Total	**2 520**	**2 610**	**3 620**

TABLE 6.7 *Annual total costs per capita for elderly populations*

Community	£	Residential homes	£	Long-stay geriatric hospital	£
(i) Not on margin	1 280–1 440*	(i) Not on margin	2 610	(i) Least dependent	5 900
(ii) On residential home margin	1 770–1 840*	(ii) On community margin	2 520	(ii) Most dependent	7 400
(iii) On hospital margin	1 490–1 650*	(iii) On hospital margin	3 620	(iii) Average	7 200
(iv) Average	1 380–1 530*	(iv) Average	2 790		

* Plus unquantified social costs (These will be present, but to a much lesser extent, in the other two locations as well)

precise as possible. For example, to obtain more accurate estimates of costs of general practitioners' services, and the costs of the marginal populations in the residential homes, would involve special surveys in their own right. Second, not all relevant costs were calculated. The more important items missing were services used by the elderly outside their own home (although the available evidence suggested that these were likely to be small); the cost of voluntary visiting; and the costs falling on relatives and friends. Overall these omissions meant that the community costs were likely to be underestimated.

The data that were obtained in this particular study suggested that for *those close to relevant boundaries of care* it was relatively more costly to care for the elderly in residential homes (about £2500) than at home (£1770 to £1840); and that it was considerably more costly to care for the elderly in hospital (about £5900) compared with in a residential home (£3620).

However, elderly people in geriatric wards were not included in the survey and it might be that even the group with the lowest nursing dependency in hospital were more dependent than the groups in the community or residential homes who were placed on the hospital margin. Given also that some domiciliary costs were not quantified, the differences for comparable margins might not have been as great as the study data suggest. Certainly, as Table 6.7 indicates, they were not as great as would be indicated if the costs used had been for the averages of the populations and not for the marginal populations.

Alternative patterns of care

Given the data from the surveys on characteristics of the different marginal populations and the costs associated with those populations it was then possible to begin to look at alternative patterns of care. The costs presented have been based on units of 60 beds or places. The reason for this is that if new geriatric beds or new residential home places are provided, then they are normally of this size. The cost figures are thus specific to this size of increase. If increments other than 60 or multiples of 60 were to be considered, then the cost estimates might vary. Again, if there were to be decreases, then different cost estimates (in this instance estimates of cost savings) would almost certainly apply.

From the cost data, it can be stated that for the same cost (of £255 000 per annum) at least three options are open to the decision-makers. (For community costs, assumption (2) has been used here for housing costs.)

(1) Open 60 new geriatric beds (at a cost of £354 000) and move 60 clients from the community into these beds (saving, in the community, £99 000): total net cost £255 000.

(2) Open 86 new geriatric beds (at a cost per annum of £507 000) and move 86 clients from residential homes into these beds (saving, in the residential homes, £311 000); then move 86 clients from the community (saving, in the community, £158 000) to the residential homes (at a cost of £217 000): total net cost £225 000.

(3) Open 375 new residential home places (at a cost per annum of £945 000) and move 375 clients from the community (a saving, in the community, of £690 000): total net cost £255 000.

(The figures emerging here are a little different from those in Mooney [47] largely because of improvements made in the estimates of hospital costs.)

Obviously, given the limitations of the cost data expressed previously, the figures emerging for the three options of 60, 86 and 375 have to be treated somewhat tentatively. (They are also – as the arithmetic works out – not all multiples of 60!) None the less they indicate how the cost data on marginal analysis can be used to show the choices open to the decision-makers. Of course it might be that they would prefer some expansion involving a mix of the options but the appropriate data could be presented to show relevant trade-offs for different mixes.

But what about the data collected on the characteristics of the marginal populations? In deciding which option to choose the decision-makers would have been presented with a picture of the type of people who would be involved in such moves, that is, the marginal populations. They are thus better able to judge, in the light of these pictures, which option to choose, but it must be emphasised that they have to form a judgement of the relative benefits of the different options.

For example in trying to decide whether to move 60 community clients to geriatric hospital or 375 community clients to residential home (each of which options costs £255 000), the decision-makers would look to Table 6.2 and 6.3 which provide information about the types of clients who would be involved in such moves.

If both options appear equally desirable then they are implying that the benefit of moving one community client to hospital is equal to the benefit of moving 6.25 (in theory!) community clients to a residential home. (The 6.25 figure is derived by dividing 375 by 60.) If they choose the former then they are implying that the benefit of the move to hospital is greater than 6.25 times the move to a residential home; a choice of the latter implies that the move to hospital is less than 6.25 times the move to a residential home. In other words marginal analysis provides relevant cost and dependency data which compel the decision-makers to be explicit about the relative implied values they are using.

Conclusion

The purpose of applying marginal analysis is to set out the marginal costs and implied marginal benefits of services which can then be comparatively valued by planners when choosing what they hope will be the most efficient allocation of scarce resources. Having demonstrated that the technique can be applied to health care, certainly at least to different types of facility for long-term support of elderly people, it would be very satisfying for the researchers to be able also to demonstrate the effect which the approach had on the planning decisions. Unfortunately, it is almost impossible to distinguish the contribution of individual sets of information without close observation, if not psychoanalysis, of the relevant discussions and discussants. However, it is difficult to believe that in the absence of marginal analysis the decision-makers could have had the relevant data to hand on which to be forced to make their relative values explicit. (Certainly, using the approach as a 'planning game' on courses for health board members, the authors have found that marginal analysis has had a considerable influence on the choices made.) Of course, the same problem could have been posed with data about averages but the equivalences of facilities which could be made available from a fixed additional resource, and the nature of the people who might benefit, would have been positively misleading.

Thus, the authors believe that, although precise, comprehensive costing, which is more desirable for marginal analysis than for programme budgeting, has not yet been obtained and the individual margins may not be homogeneous, the study has demonstrated both the feasibility and the relevance of the technique in focusing on the people likely to be affected by a shift in resources. We are therefore at a loss to understand the recent unexpanded comment by Knapp [40] that this approach 'needs further development before it can claim to be a sufficiently valid, realistic and sensitive tool to warrant widescale employment'. It is not perfect; but we are confident that its benefits easily outweigh its costs, accepting of course that this is a subjective judgement. While the emphasis in this chapter has been on care of the elderly, marginal analysis is applicable to any programme where alternative patterns of care are being considered – and indeed in forming judgements about the balance of care between programmes.

7

Some Case Studies in the Application of Cost–Effectiveness and Cost–Benefit Analysis

In chapter 4 the evaluative techniques of cost–effectivness analysis and cost–benefit analysis were outlined. Most studies claiming to use these techniques in health care have in practice involved cost–effectiveness analysis, that is investigating *how* to deliver health care, rather than cost–benefit analysis, in which the emphasis is more on *whether and how much* of different types of care to provide.

A short bibliography of some of these analyses is provided at the end of the book and the reader who is interested in the application of the techniques to a particular problem would be well advised to follow up relevant references. The main purpose of this chapter is to examine certain aspects of a few of such studies and draw some broad lessons from them. It is not intended as a comprehensive guide to applying cost–effectiveness and cost–benefit analysis; for that readers are referred to Drummond [24]. None the less this book would be incomplete without a comment on some of the attributes and some of the pitfalls. The studies have been chosen to highlight various aspects of economic appraisal in action, some based on work undertaken in the authors' department. The studies are described in two ways: first, a description of the health service topic covered; and second, the economic issues exemplified.

The sixth stool guaiac

Marginal costing and implied values

A much quoted study by Neuhauser and Lewicki [50] serves to highlight two important aspects of the economic evaluation techniques outlined: first, the importance of *marginal* cost and, second, the importance of implied values.

One test which has been advocated for the detection of asymptomatic colonic cancer is testing of stools for the presence of occult blood. Greegor [33] has suggested a protocol of six sequential tests since an isolated test may be negative even where colonic cancer exists.

Neuhauser and Lewicki constructed the following table (Table 7.1) on the basis of:

(1) a population of 10 000 of whom 72 have colonic cancer; and
(2) each guaiac test detecting 91.67 per cent of cases of cancer undetected by the previous test. (Thus the first test detects 91.67 per cent of total cases; the second, 91.67 per cent of the 8.33 per cent undetected by the first test, that is 7.64 per cent; and so on.)

Neuhauser and Lewicki then estimated the costs of screening against the number of cases detected. This is shown in Table 7.2 from which it can be seen that as each successive set of tests is

TABLE 7.1   *True positive rates and numbers of cases in population of 10 000 of whom 72 have colonic cancer with sequential guaiac tests*

	True positive results	
Number of sets of tests	%	*Number of cases*
1	91.6667	65.9469
2	99.3056	71.4424
3	99.9421	71.9003
4	99.9952	71.9385
5	99.9996	71.9417
6	99.9999	71.9420

TABLE 7.2 *Numbers of cases detected and costs ($) of screening with sequential guaiac tests*

Number of sets of tests	Total cases detected	Total costs* $	Average costs† $
1	65.9469	77 511	1 175
2	71.4424	107 690	1 507
3	71.9003	130 199	1 811
4	71.9385	148 116	2 059
5	71.9417	163 141	2 268
6	71.9420	176 331	2 451

* Costs include the cost of guaiac stool tests on 10 000 population plus the cost of barium-enema examinations on all those found positive
† Total cost divided by number of true positive cases detected

carried out the total costs rise but, because each results in successively fewer *new* positive tests which have to be followed up by barium enema examination, the incremental costs of each set of tests falls. (For example the cost of the second set of tests is $30 179 whereas for the sixth set it is $13 190.) The *average* cost (that is total cost divided by total cases detected) increases with each successive set of tests because total costs increase faster than do total cases detected. However, the average cost does little more than double from the first to the sixth set of tests.

But, in deciding how many tests to carry out, the data presented above are potentially misleading because, as Neuhauser and Lewicki indicate, it is the *marginal* cost per case detected which is relevant to the decision on how many tests to apply (that is the cost of detecting one extra case by each sequential test).

The data from Table 7.2 can be revamped into the more appropriate form indicated in Table 7.3. From Table 7.3 it can now be seen that the marginal costs differ markedly (except for the first test of course) from the average costs. For the sixth test, in this example the incremental cost is over $13 000 and the marginal cost over $47 million.

Clearly Neuhauser and Lewicki's results are heavily dependent on their assumptions about prevalence and sensitivity (that is the percentage of positives detected which are true). However, the study serves as an excellent example of the importance of deter-

TABLE 7.3   *Incremental cases detected and incremental and marginal costs*
($) of sequential guaiac tests

Number of sets of tests	Incremental cases detected	Incremental costs $	Marginal cost* $
1	65.9469	77 511	1 175
2	5.4956	30 179	5 492
3	0.4580	22 509	49 150
4	0.0382	17 917	469 534
5	0.0032	15 024	4 724 695
6	0.0003	13 190	47 107 214

* The marginal cost is the incremental cost divided by the incremental cases detected (that is, it is the additional cost of the nth test divided by the additional cases detected by the nth test)

mining marginal cost. Compare the following two statements, both true and both drawn from exactly the same data:

(a) with six sequential tests the average cost per case detected is $2451;
(b) with six sequential tests the marginal cost per case detected is over $47 million.

Given the first statement, it might appear not unreasonable to go ahead with a screening programme of six tests. However, the second, more appropriate, statement would presumably cast doubts on whether a six-test programme should be mounted and would promote an enquiry about the value of even a five- or four-test programme.

Thus Table 7.3 provides a good example of the concept of implied values. If the American Cancer Society, which has endorsed a protocol of six sequential tests, has now seen the work of Neuhauser and Lewicki it is difficult to believe that they will not have rethought their endorsement of all six tests – particularly if they bear in mind that resources are limited. More important, it can now ask itself the question – is it worth paying over $47 million to detect one case of colonic cancer? If not, that rules out the sixth sequential test. The question is then posed: is it worth paying $4.7 million (the marginal cost in the fifth test)? If not, that rules out the fifth sequential test; and so on until the position is reached, albeit subjectively, that the benefits of detecting one positive case outweigh the marginal costs involved.

In the context of the NHS, similar analyses of policy options can be conducted. In this way decision-making becomes more explicit and in the fullness of time more rational. The rationality will follow when sufficient studies are mounted that the marginal costs of similar outputs can be equated across different policy areas.

Child-proof drug containers

Implied values

In 1971 the Minister of Health announced that the government would not be proceeding with the child proofing of drug containers on grounds of cost. In an article in *New Scientist*, Gould [30] examined this decision and put forward some interesting, if rough and ready, figures which serve to highlight the importance of looking at implied values in health policy making. (While the assumptions used are grossly over-simplified, it is the principles involved which are important.) Gould's argument was essentially this. About 60 children die each year as a result of swallowing various medicaments. In addition, about 16 000 children are admitted to hospital either because they have, or are thought to have, swallowed certain medical preparations.

Now if it is assumed (as it was by Gould) that the cost of drug proofing per annum was £500 000 and the cost per in-patient episode was £30, it becomes possible to estimate the implied value of a child's life. This is done as follows:

Cost of drug proofing	£500 000
Cost of 16 000 child admissions at £30 each	£480 000
Net cost	£20 000

Forgetting the non-fatal morbidity involved for the children and assuming that a third of the 60 deaths could be averted by child proofing, these figures imply that the government was not prepared to make a net outlay of £20 000 to save the lives of 20 children. Thus the implied value of a child's life was less than £1000.

While it is possible to question the accuracy of Gould's figures and his assumptions this provides a further simple, if crude, example of implied values. Ideally it is the implied marginal value that is required but for this particular policy the average and marginal values may well be equal. It could be of course that different methods of child proofing are available and that their effectiveness differs. If this were so then it would be possible to obtain implied marginal values for the various methods.

Breast cancer screening

CEA and multiple outputs

This study [64] on breast cancer screening highlights the limitations of cost–effectiveness analysis when the choice faced is that of 'how' (for example, how should a breast cancer screening regime be conducted?) but there is more than one output from the programme.

In any screening programme there are four outputs – true positives and negatives and false positives and negatives. A true positive is a case which is screened as likely to have the disease and a subsequent test (in the case of breast cancer, a biopsy) confirms it. A true negative is where the test indicates that disease is absent and in fact it is. A false positive is where a positive screen is subsequently shown by a biopsy to be 'false' – disease is not present. A false negative occurs in a woman who is told from the screen she is OK when in fact she has the disease.

True positives and true negatives are 'good' things. The former will normally allow earlier more effective treatment and the latter reassures the women that they are clear. The false results are 'bad' things: a false positive means extra resource costs for an 'unnecessary' biopsy and anxiety for the woman; a false negative may mean a delay in presenting symptomatically just because the woman has been told she is clear (with possibly poorer prognosis than if presentation had been earlier).

Simpson, Gravelle and Chamberlain [64] examined a number of different ways of screening for breast cancer for their sensitivity (that is their ability to identify diseased cases accurately), their specificity (that is their ability to identify non-diseased cases accurately) and their cost. Given what has been said above, high sensitivity and high specificity are both good things. However, sensitivity and specificity tend to move in opposite directions.

This means that while some tests can be eliminated from consideration on the basis of information indicating that they are more costly and have no greater sensitivity/specificity than some other test, some other way needs to be found to make a choice between the remaining tests. The authors suggest that this is best done by means of explicitly placing money values on the four different outcomes and establishing what the best buy is in terms of the expected net value of each test. This is done by fitting such values into an expression which reads as follows:

$$\beta_1 P \pi_1 + B_2(1-P)(1-\pi_2) + B_3 P(1-\pi_1) + B_4(1-P)\pi_2 - C$$

And where π_1 = sensitivity
π_2 = specificity
P = prevalence
B_1 = value assigned to true positive
B_2 = value assigned to false positive
B_3 = value assigned to false negative
B_4 = value assigned to true negative
C = cost of test

While it might be possible to take cost–effectiveness further than these authors imply by this approach (see the second example of breast cancer screening below), none the less it does remain the case that multiple outputs do create difficulties for the cost–effectiveness analyst. Also worth noting in this example is that the authors did ask a small sample of community medicine specialists to choose between the tests, all of whom experienced some difficulty and indeed in many cases got it wrong in terms of choosing on efficiency grounds. This suggests that such an analytical approach as was adopted by these researchers can prove useful to the making of policy choices.

Duodenal ulcer treatment

Clinical and economic evaluation, valuing life, discounting and sensitivity analysis

Despite the plethora of clinical trials of drugs, concern about rising drug expenditures, drug safety (for example, thalidomide and practolol) and restricted lists, there are still relatively few studies which attempt to bring together clinical and economic evaluation of drugs and drug therapies. However, one attempt to do so was by Culyer and Maynard [10] for the treatment of duodenal ulcers, where one choice of treatment involved the drug cimetidine, and the other, surgery.

The study draws attention to two key issues in any evaluative analysis. In posing the fundamental question about whether something is worth doing, two questions immediately follow: first, 'worthwhile relative to what alternative?', and 'worthwhile to whom?'

On the first of these, although claiming to be a cost–effectiveness study one of the most interesting aspects of this research is that the authors had great difficulty in establishing from the existing literature at the time (1981) what the relative effectiveness of the different regimes was. Indeed there have been few studies 'which compare cimetidine treatment with alternatives such as "do nothing" (self-healing), an intensive antacid regimen or truncal vagotomy'. The authors attempted to overcome this difficulty by using sensitivity analysis and always loading their calculations *against* cimetidine (so that if it still came out 'on top' it could be fairly certain that it was justified that it did so).

One of the main problems in using economic appraisal is highlighted in this study and at the same time one of the main deficiencies in current clinical evaluations. The authors point to the fact that commonly clinical trials make 'no systematic comparison of effectiveness of cimetidine with alternative treatments' and restrict their concern to the basic question 'does the treatment (with cimetidine) have benefit, or do harm?' (usually by comparison with placebo).

On the question of 'worthwhile to whom'?, this study highlights the fact that economic appraisal is concerned with social costs and social benefits so that any such analysis ought to be set against the broadest of backgrounds. While that is the *intention* of such appraisal exercises, often (and this is a case in point) intentions and realities tend to part!

It is the costing in this study which is of particular interest. For vagotomy these are presented in Table 7.4 (based on Culyer and Maynard's table 2).

TABLE 7.4 *Treatment of DU by vagotomy. Cost per case (1978 prices)*

	Lowest estimate (£)	Highest estimate (£)
Ward costs	340	350
Operating costs	30	50
Differential patient costs	580	970
Value of risk of death	230	15 000
Total cost per case	**1 180**	**16 370**

Differential patient costs related solely to the value of the lost output associated with patients' absence from work. The figures should ideally include pain, suffering, etc., and costs to relatives and friends.

The costs of risk of death are interesting. Clearly there *is* such a risk in undergoing a vagotomy; equally clearly it does represent a cost in that the patient would prefer that the risk was lower or, better still, zero. The authors used three different ways of valuing risk of death: the values laid down elsewhere in the public sector (in this instance the Department of the Environment's value of life of £68 500); the human capital approach which values individuals in terms of their expected productive output (£46 000); and the values that individuals are willing to pay to reduce their risk of death (£3 million). Given a case-fatality rate of 0.5 per cent, these values of life give the cost of the fatality risk as £340, £230 or £15 000 respectively – proving, perhaps as we might expect, that valuing such difficult 'commodities' as human life remains a necessary but somewhat inexact science.

For cimetidine treatment, two long-term regimes were costed as in Table 7.5 (based on Culyer and Maynard's table 3).

TABLE 7.5 *Costs of two patterns[1] of long-term cimetidine treatment (£ per case, discount rate 7 per cent)*

	Duration of treatment (years)			
	20 years	25 years	30 years	35 years
Pattern 1				
Present value of first year's cost	98	98	98	98
Present value of subsequent years' cost	911	1 011	1 082	1 132
Total	**1 009**	**1 109**	**1 180**	**1 230**
Pattern 2				
Present value of first year's cost	107	107	107	107
Present value of subsequent years' cost	911	1 011	1 082	1 132
Total	**1 018**	**1 118**	**1 189**	**1 239**

1. Pattern 1: 1000 mg per day for 4 weeks; 400 mg per day thereafter
   Pattern 2: 1000 mg per day for 6 weeks; 40 mg per day thereafter

This table gives a neat example of both sensitivity analysis and discounting. (Indeed the authors also applied sensitivity analysis to the discount rate, with the original table also providing figures for a 5 per cent and a 10 per cent discount rate.)

In summary, the study found that the lowest estimates of cost per case were £1180 for vagotomy and £1010 for cimetidine and the highest £16 370 and £1240 respectively. While entering various caveats, the authors conclude that they judge 'the drug treatment to be substantially less costly than surgery for DU where the choice is clinically acceptable'.

One final point is worth making on this study. The viewpoint does matter in many instances and particularly in this case. Culyer and Maynard state that 'from the point of view of the NHS ... surgery seems the cheaper alternative whereas from the wider, community, perspective surgery is relatively inexpensive.' Economic appraisal would always press for the latter viewpoint to be endorsed since the form for such appraisal is not restricted to health services' resource use but society's at large.

Provision of acute beds

Equity, efficiency and implied values

Equity has only been but mentioned in this book and it is not the intention to discuss it in detail here. However, in the specific context of economic appraisal studies it is pertinent to mention the case of the Fife District General Hospital.

This study by Henderson *et al*. [34] was one of several being conducted in the NHS using what is officially known as 'Option Appraisal' [4] but is in effect simply economic appraisal. It is now obligatory throughout the UK that for various schemes, especially major capital schemes, health boards/authorities must conduct an option appraisal exercise before they will be given approval by health departments to proceed with the scheme.

As part of this process, an option appraisal study was conducted on the question of the poor quality and low number of acute beds in Fife. A number of options were examined for dealing with this problem, most of which involved some expansion of the existing acute beds in Fife itself but one of which resulted in *increased* cross boundary flows of patients from Fife into Edinburgh hospitals in the adjoining Lothian Health Board.

One of the major issues that arose in this study was the question of efficiency versus equity. The most efficient solution to Fife's problems appeared to be to have substantial cross boundary flows to Edinburgh hospitals. This arose largely because of the existing spare capacity in acute beds in Edinburgh and the resultant low marginal costs (the relevant costs) for treating additional Fife patients in Edinburgh. In other words the overheads are already there in Edinburgh; if more beds were built in Fife overheads would have to be met.

But is it equitable to have patients travelling outside their own area? Option or economic appraisal cannot answer this question but it can provide the appropriate information on which a rational decision can be made. As Henderson states: 'If everybody could be made better off by an option then it would be efficient. One implication of the difference in cost between Option A [the Edinburgh option] and B [the best Fife option] is that the NHS would still save money even if it were to pay £500 compensation to every patient who had to travel to Edinburgh. If these patients preferred hospital treatment in Edinburgh plus £500 to hospital treatment in a new hospital in Dunfermline [in Fife], then everybody would be better off if the £500 compensation were paid, and so Option A would be the efficient option.'

This position was further complicated by the fact that cross boundary flows under SHARE (the Scottish RAWP) are costed at *average* cost. This meant in effect that while Lothian could treat Fife patients at a *marginal* cost of £12 per day, Fife were paying Lothian around £70 per day for such cases. Indeed to have a substantial increase in the cross boundary flow *at average costs* would have meant that Fife could not within its anticipated budget have afforded to send all the patients to Edinburgh. Thus even if on efficiency grounds the Edinburgh option were selected as best and the equity weight not taken to be as high as £500 per patient travelling, the inappropriate nature of the costing of cross boundary flows (i.e. average rather than marginal costing) means that the efficiency option might not be able to be afforded by Fife Health Board.

All of which in a sense suggests that using economic appraisal more may highlight not only more efficient and equitable answers to specific problems but also help to improve the organisational rules under which the NHS operates.

Congenital toxoplasmosis

Sensitivity analysis and CBA

This study [35] exemplifies very neatly two important features of economic appraisal in health care: first, the desirability of any such study involving not just an economist but other disciplines; and, second, the use of sensitivity analysis when there are doubts about the accuracy of some of the data or the assumptions that have to be used.

The study arose because of an interest in the subject of toxoplasmosis by a group of medical staff at the University of Sheffield who contacted a health economist (Henderson) after reading his previous related work on screening for spina bifida. It is an excellent example of the way in which open co-operation can lead to useful evaluation studies combining the relevant medical, epidemiological and economic skills.

The paper demonstrates how, even in the absence of hard data on the incidence of congenital toxoplasmosis, the extent of the harm it causes through mental and visual handicaps and the effectiveness of preventive measures, none the less an economic evaluation can still be productively conducted.

The value of 'sensitivity analysis' comes over strongly in this paper. The authors state: 'If . . . a service has not been practised widely or for long, much of the empirical evidence necessary for accurate analysis may not have emerged. As it may well be inefficient to delay consideration of services until margins of uncertainty have been minimised . . . the technique of sensitivity analysis can be used to try to overcome this problem.'

The main focus of the authors' evaluative study is the possible introduction of a serological surveillance, say, for toxoplasma infection in pregnant women and its prophylactic treatment – in other words a screening service. Congenital toxoplasma infection can cause visual and mental disabilities and even death. However, 'the main benefit of [a screening service], the reduction in the harmful effects of congenital toxoplasma infection, cannot be estimated with any degree of confidence because the reported clinical and epidemiological data are generally based on studies of relatively small numbers of cases'.

From the limited data available the researchers calculated that the annual incidence of congenital toxoplasmosis lay between 50 and 500 with a best estimate of 150. From this they calculate that the resultant annual incidence of mental retardation will lie between 30 and 300 with a best estimate of 90, and of visual handicap between 40 and 400 with a best estimate of 120.

On preventable costs the authors included costs of institutional care, extra expenses to the family, special education, loss of marketed output, operations for strabismus, ophthalmic out-patient attendances and acute hospital care. (They did not include the intangible benefits of preventing the neonatal deaths or of preventing handicap to those affected, their families and others concerned. Henderson previously had calculated that parents appear willing to bear costs of some £15 000 to have a child, and the authors have suggested that 'a sum of this magnitude might

represent the value of the intangible benefit to parents of preventing mental retardation'. If it did they suggest that the incorpora-
tion of such a figure in their estimations would not alter the
conclusions of their study.)

The costs that might be prevented by a screening service were
estimated at £4.8 million with a minimum and maximum of £1.6
million and £15.9 million respectively.

Using two different methods of screening and including subsequent treatment the costs of a screening service were estimated at
either £4.73 million ± £2.37 million or £11.53 million ± £5.77
million. Data on effectivness of treatment are particularly poor
and here the authors had to assume levels of effectiveness of 25 per
cent, 50 per cent and 75 per cent.

What emerges from all this? Well despite the 'ifs' and 'buts' and
doubts and uncertainties, the researchers did make some sense of
the very rough information on which they had to work. Their
findings are presented in Table 7.6.

TABLE 7.6   *Tangible benefits (preventable costs): £million (discounted @
5%)*

		Incidence estimates		
		Minimum	Central	Maximum
Effectiveness	75%	1.19	3.58	11.93
(% reduction in	50%	0.80	2.39	7.95
incidence)	25%	0.40	1.19	3.98

Thus even at the lower cost estimate for the surveillance
programme the authors concluded that 'only if the incidence of
congenital toxoplasmosis were at the maximum end of our range
and if a screening service could prevent around half of all cases,
would the tangible benefit outweigh the most likely cost estimate.'

But they didn't stop there. They drew comparison with the
possible costs and benefits of a health education campaign and
suggested that this would be less costly and 'would be more likely
to save resources'.

Their conclusions are tentative, as the authors are at pains to point out – but they are useful in pointing out in what direction research should go in this field. Further, sensitivity analysis has allowed these researchers 'to show what conditions would have to hold to justify a screening service or health education campaign on the grounds that its benefits exceeded its costs'. This is no small achievement for such a simple and easily applied tool.

Breast cancer screening (again)

Handling intangible costs, limits of cost–effectiveness analysis

One of the authors was involved in a study of breast cancer screening in Edinburgh [49]. This study attempted to address the question of 'which screening test', solely on the basis of cost–effectiveness analysis, and overcame at least some of the problems identified by Simpson, Gravelle and Chamberlain [64] as outlined above.

This study argued that the resource and anxiety costs associated with a false positive were unknown, but called them £x. Similarly the costs of a false negative were unknown but called £y. Consequently the total costs, cancers detected and costs per cancer detected for the programmes investigated were as in Table 7.7.

If (as the study did) we ignore the value of reassurance, then we can see that whatever the value of x and y, the least cost per cancer detected is in the third programme – that is, mammography plus clinical examination. However, if we assume a positive value of £z for the value of reassurance for a true negative we do not have as certain an outcome for the selection of the most cost–effective programme.

It is clearly the case from this example that there will be occasions, particularly when we have more than one output from a programme, that the apparently straightforward separation of cost–benefit analysis from cost–effectiveness will become blurred.

110   *Choices for Health Care*

TABLE 7.7   *Total costs and cost–effectiveness for different screening regimes*

	Mammography, thermography and clinical examination	Thermography and clinical examination	Mammography and clinical examination
Single reporting and 1 clinical examination			
(a) Total cost	£53 700 + £8x + £92.5y	£43 000 + £12.5x + £71y	£43 600 + £8x + £92.5y
(b) Cancers detected	12	7.5	12
(c) Cost per cancer detected	£4500 + £0.7x + £7.7y	£5700 + £1.7x + £9.5y	£3600 + £0.7x + £7.7y

Motorway crash barriers

Non-health-care health

While not strictly in the field of health policy, the issue of motorway crash barriers provides a useful example of the application of cost–benefit analysis to the saving of life and prevention of injury. The problem here was that vehicles on motorways occasionally crossed the central reserve and collided with vehicles on the other carriageway. Would it be justified to erect barriers on the central reserves of motorways (the 'whether worthwhile' question of cost–benefit analysis) and if so, on which motorways should they be erected (the 'how much' question of cost–benefit analysis)?

A study group in the Department of Environment obtained data on the effectiveness of motorway barriers by studying the accident records of two stretches of the M1 – one section having a barrier and the other not. The classification of accidents was such that the effect of the barrier could be estimated. The difference between the expected accidents and the recorded accidents on the section with the barrier provided an estimate of the effectiveness of the barrier. Applying Dawson's [11] accident cost figures, the cost of the accidents arising because of the absence of barriers was estimated and thereby the benefits of erecting barriers. The ratio of benefit to cost was estimated to be 4.2 for a dual three lane road with an average daily flow of 30 000 vehicles. At this level of flow, since the ratio of benefits to costs exceeded unity, the cost–benefit study pointed to the implementation of barrier erection.

This particular case is an interesting one from several points of view. First, in order to detemine effectiveness a controlled trial had to be mounted. Without knowledge of effectiveness, it is difficult for the cost–benefit analyst to make progress. Second, because of the nature of the effect of installing barriers the values used in the cost–benefit study were extremely important. For example, at low traffic volumes, barriers can increase the risk of an accident or increase the severity. This arises because if the barrier had not been erected there would be a high probability that a vehicle could cross the reserve and not collide with another vehicle. Thus the higher the traffic volume the higher the benefit from barriers. Further, the main benefit from barriers is in reducing fatal accidents but they may result in an increase in non-fatal accidents. There is therefore a potential trade-off between a relatively small number of fatal accidents avoided and a somewhat larger number of additional non-fatal accidents. In such a trade-off the relative values attached to fatal and non-fatal accidents become crucial.

Partly as a result of this study, but also because of pressure from the media and the public, the Minister stated in 1971 that a programme to erect barriers on about 1000 miles of motorway by 1975 would be begun. Thus the cost–benefit analysis study in this case not only provided guidance on *whether* or not barriers should be erected but also, because of the differential levels of benefit with different traffic volumes, *where* barriers should be erected and hence *how many* miles of barrier were desirable.

Conclusion

Various aspects of the case studies outlined in this chapter have been highlighted in order to give the reader a 'feel' for the application of cost–effectiveness and cost–benefit analysis. Clearly it has not been possible to report these studies in as much detail as they merit and the reader is advised to examine the studies in more detail together with some of the others listed in the short bibliography at the end of the book.

In addition before attempting to undertake cost–effectiveness or cost–benefit studies for himself, the reader would do well to make himself familiar with Drummond's [24] guide to the application of these techniques.

8

An Introduction to the National Health Service

The National Health Service itself has evolved from an ideal and during the evolution the expectations and attitudes of the originators, the patients, the public at large and indeed the staff of the service have changed.

There is no doubt that in 1948 new hospitals and renovations were necessary and the building programme that resulted concentrated an undue amount of activity into those services where the needs were most obvious, as opposed to perhaps most pressing, or in those services which had the ability to utilise money quickly. So great were the deficiencies at the time that the thought of an appropriate balance between various services was far from people's minds. Since then comprehensive planning in the health service has been inhibited by the increase in recurrent money, certainly up until the early 1970s, and the considerable capital investments that have been made over the years. Thus, instead of the distribution being later adjusted, those services whose buildings, and therefore facilities and opportunities for training, were available first have continued to grow and those starting later, in terms of access to recurrent monies and opportunities to attract staff and develop their specialty, have remained handicapped.

The emphasis on the building programme which then determined the services, rather than on the services which ought to have determined the building programme, has led to the charge of disjointed incrementalism and currently proposed capital buildings programmes still seek specifically to redress the balance [60].

It is possible with hindsight to criticise the early planning priorities and indeed the type of planning undertaken and although attempts were made to redistribute resources [15, 59, 62]

113

the actual shift was minimal. Indeed one of the first requirements should have been to develop the appropriate planning facilities and skills which, as a result of those decisions, had been neglected. This will involve not merely acquiring staff with the necessary experience but also a change in attitude and understanding on the part of many people in the health service. It is not the purpose of the remaining chapters to describe in detail the structure and functioning of the health service but rather to indicate the inter-relationships and attitudes of the professional groups and the various administrative procedures through which the application of both the principles and techniques of any new planning proce-dures must be promoted.

There have recently been two major initiatives in health service management: first, the removal of an entire administrative tier [19] with a greater delegation of responsibility to units actually deliver-ing the services to patients; and second, the introduction of general managers [20] with inevitable consequences for consensus management. The full implications of these changes will take some time to work through the system and this chapter therefore is confined to an overview of the operation of the service and the various groups involved in decision-making and planning are described. In chapter 10 the contribution of health economics to planning and the possibility of consequent changes in the opera-tion of the service are discussed.

The National Health Service

The size of the health service is not always fully appreciated but three simple statistics [5] give an indication of the scale. First, over 200 million visits are made each year by people to general practitioners; second, 30 million contacts either as in-patients or out-patients are made with the hospital service; and, third, 1 person in every 25 of the working population is employed by the health service.

It is inevitable that, in a service that has evolved to encompass nearly 250 million annual transactions and a work force of over 1.2 million, the variations that have arisen in planning, control, and day-to-day management are difficult to disentangle and describe. Obviously, certain features are common to all the various functional and geographical components of the health-care system in this country but such is the range of these functions and areas that without some measure of flexibility the service could not operate. As a result of a compromise between those arrangements subject to national uniformity and those options determined by the constraints of local circumstance, the impression of a complex and somewhat haphazard organisation has been created. It is, therefore, pertinent to define the various groups involved, the public as well as the practitioners, and to indicate the nature of their contributions, interactions and expectations, since without some knowledge of the setting it is difficult to appreciate the possibilities for implementing economic techniques.

Any attempt at a brief description covering such a wide range of activities and people is likely to do less than justice to individual services and the main emphasis must be on those features which either promote or inhibit the running of the service. When the health service started it was divided, in terms of policy and finance, into three parts: the general practitioner services (dental, medical, ophthalmic and pharmaceutical), the local authority preventive services and the hospital or specialist services. Of all the changes since the inauguration of the health services, unquestionably the biggest and most significant were those associated with the attempted integration of these original three branches.

In 1948 the health service was faced with three major problems. First, there had been insufficient investment particularly in hospitals; second, there was unequal access to health care; and, third, there was no measure of the extent and nature of need for individual services. There was little conflict between the health-care professions and the government on ultimate aims but there was considerable dispute over the means of achieving them [29]. In the end the compromise structure was agreed, with general practitioners remaining independent contractors, with hospital staff joining a salaried service and with local authorities transferring their hospitals but retaining the services which they themselves had created to compensate for the existing inequalities in access to care. There is no question that better care resulted. Finance appeared where previously none had existed, there was a gradual redistribution of services and attempts were made to develop services to meet community needs. By these means over the first ten to fifteen years the health service achieved a measure of geographical, financial and social equalisation in respect of access to services.

Despite these improvements each of the aims of the original service ran into its own particular set of problems. Adequate financing was affected by increased demand, by improved methods and standards of care and by raised expectations. Redistribution of services was foiled by some intractable problems such as less attractive areas in which to work, urban and rural differences, teaching and non-teaching centres and articulate or less articulate patients, to mention but a few. Meeting needs in its turn was haphazard through lack of early planning control, lack of information and competition at government level with non-health service priorities.

For these reasons it was argued that the health service would be even more successful if its organisational divisions were removed so that competition between individual services would be reduced, priorities would be agreed and developments co-ordinated. The three original problems of finance, distribution and need still remained but, with reorganisation of the health service, were to be tackled in a slightly different way. The objectives of integration in 1974 were, first, to simplify administration by allowing better assessment and quicker reallocation of resources; second, to provide scarce or expensive services on a national scale; and, third, to achieve closer contact and consultation with the public, the staff and professions, and local government.

The reorganisation of 1982 was primarily concerned with health service management. This concern had been manifest in the Report of the Royal Commission, was foreshadowed by the 1976 Three Chairmen's Enquiry into the DHSS, with the resulting Körner Group on health services information, and was finally sealed by the independent NHS Management Inquiry of 1983 [18, 20, 54]. The emphasis was on the need for devolution of power and a greater influence by the consumer, and these were to be achieved by a simplification of the structure, by performance reviews and by greater accountability to Parliament. The NHS has in most respects proved to be a success. The criticisms levelled at the service are neither serious nor unique. Virtually every other health care system faces similar problems and few have resolved them as satisfactorily. The real problem is the struggle for power being waged within the service and the resulting desperate attempts to find an appropriate means of management. Such conflicts are inevitable and as pointed out by Virchow more than a hundred years ago 'health is but politics writ large'. The important matters therefore are not the structure, the organisation or the management, but the people, their values, their needs and their relationships.

An overview of the service

There can be few large organisations which if examined in detail by an uninvolved observer would not be found to be deficient and illogical. Such is the nature of progress that all the small improvements or adaptations very quickly alter the original design. Indeed it is only by producing such apparent illogicalities that man and his creations can retain the capacity to adapt to changing environments.

So it is with the health service. Its success depends primarily on the people who provide care and their ability to identify with and feel themselves a part not only of the organisation but also of the management. To achieve this the organisation has to be one that allows the people providing care to be involved not only in the efficient use of resources but also in determining the priorities for the best distribution of these resources. Accommodating a true representation of a workforce of 1.2 million is in itself a formidable undertaking; when set alongside the potentially conflicting requirement of effective management to maintain a limit on health care expenditure and to ensure that the necessarily limited resources are utilised as effectively as possible, the task and the structure become Herculean. The reorganised structure in 1974 was an attempt to allow participation at all levels but without a functional framework for conflicting aims to be openly discussed.

The 1982 reorganisation was an attempt to simplify the structure and strengthen management. Readers unfamiliar with the service and wishing more background should refer to a detailed account of the changes in organisation [51].

The cornerstone of health service organisation is the district health authority or area board which is responsible for health care in geographical area corresponding as nearly as possible to those of local authority regions and districts. Ultimately there is corporate responsibility to the English Department of Health and Social Security, the Scottish Home and Health Department, the Welsh Office or Northern Ireland's Ministry of Health and Social Services. In effect, by means of delegated authority to the various tiers, there is a progression from broad policy, through intermediate planning and control to detailed implementation at the periphery. This is achieved by a multidisciplinary grouping for executive, planning and some advisory functions at virtually all levels of the organisation. These principles apply generally although there are slight differences in all four countries.

Control of the health service therefore is exercised through the appropriate Secretary of State, whose staff in the respective departments translate the policy laid down by Parliament into instructions, guidelines and ultimately resources. These, in turn, are administered by health authorities or boards, the membership of which has been determined by the Secretary of State. The organisation of the health service within virtually autonomous health authorities is based primarily on the function or services which the various categories of staff are required to perform or operate.

Staff interactions within authorities

Quite separate in terms of origin and indeed ultimate function, and in no way part of the basic or fiscal organisation of the health service, are the professional and craft groupings which after a long process of evolution are now essential for the purposes of training, the maintenance of standards, and the collective welfare of the members of the group. As in so many other industries serving as they do various professions and trades, these groupings do not fit within a single structure nor, for example in the cases of nurses, doctors and therapists, are they necessarily interrelated. Because the purpose is akin to that of a trade union or craft guild there is no direct relationship between the health service structure and the professional or trade groups. Services such as those concerned with child health, diseases of the eye, the provision of clean linen and laundry or engineering maintenance, to choose but four examples, will each contain within them members of many separate and unrelated professional and craft associations. As will emerge, this is of advantage to the health service in respect of training and standards but a problem in terms of organisation and decision-making.

In spite of this diversity the staff of health authorities can be grouped broadly under three headings namely, administration, the health-care professions and the support services. The declared management policy of the health service is now to move towards a partnership and to have at least involvement of all groups of staff in the preliminary stages of decision-making. After prolonged discussions and negotiation it was decided that the involvement of staff would be by means of their professional groupings in preference to their service commitment. For example, groups such as doctors [58] and nurses [56] in Scotland would offer independent professional advice rather than offer their advice in relation to the particular services within which they were working together as members of the same health-care teams. As a result the next requirement became some means of relating the health service's own organisation to the wholly independent professional and trade groups.

If decision-making is to be effective it must not only be explicit but explained and the various channels of communication and the groups they feed must be defined and understood by everyone involved. This was to be achieved via the existing structure within the service. Two separate streams of information sharing the same channel would be formed, one, executive and based on line management, passing on the decisions and the consequences of decisions by the health authority to the various health care and support services and the second, advisory and based on the profession and craft grouping, carrying back the concerns and advice of staff. In practice it has been found that the two streams could not be contained within the same channel and a number of additional separate channels have evolved, some passing information in both directions but others carrying only a single and occasionally turbulent stream.

The original aim was not without foundation; within the administrative structure the majority of health care and support services can certainly be identified at all levels of management. In general the channels of communication within the support services such as building and supplies are direct for, although their activities are essential to the effective running of the system, they are able to work relatively independently and are less influenced by the policies and practices of other groups than are the health care professionals. To a much greater extent those directly involved in providing health care must work as teams or in multi-professional groups and as a result the channels and processes of communication, both executive and advisory, are correspondingly interwoven. A further consequence and complication, partly because of size but partly because so many of the most senior professionals work on the factory floor, is a separation of the people concerned with the administrative and management components of the health-care professions from their colleagues who manage the support services. Thus the authority of the resulting line organisation, particularly of the more specialised health-care professionals, has been found to vary more than was expected depending on the size of the group, the degree of internal specialisation and the patterns of previous practice. This is particularly demonstrated in the case of doctors, where there is no line management and the corresponding administrative staff must therefore interact with the profession rather than speak on their behalf.

A health authority, therefore, is served by and operates through an executive group of senior officers communicating with, even identifying with, but not necessarily representing the major professional and other groups working in the service. This basic nucleus is repeated at various intermediate levels including unit to ensure an appropriate executive network. As the network extends so the responsibilities, role and composition change, initially from adminstration and policy-making to management of individual services; further out, as the day-to-day management component increases so does the involvement of health-care professional and other staff in such activities for at least a proportion of their time. Here again the effect of size is critical. At one extreme (for example, for physiotherapy) planning, management and some part of the health-care activity itself is carried out by a single individual while at the other extreme (for example, with doctors) these functions must be performed by a far greater number of people – depending on the size of a unit perhaps well over two hundred – who not only are employed in different parts of the health service's basic organisational structure but also are members of the great many professional and staff groups that exist to represent the varied interests and functions of the medical profession. Under these circumstances it is perhaps not surprising that difficulties are found in sharing a common channel of communication and a consensus on advice. Add to this the fact that medicine is but one of the advisory structures and it can then be appreciated why the business of consultation within the health service has become so complex.

The creation of advisory committees representing most of the health-care professionals was intended to let the advice from the medical profession be set and seen alongside that from the many other professional groups. There is little or no communication between the separate advisory groups so that professions working together in providing care then proffer advice independently on how resources should be distributed or developed. In part this can be explained by the lingering anxiety of the other professions, because of the previous dominance by the doctors, that without independent advisory channels their views would be subject to dilution or contradiction by medical interests. In practice, however, this apparent equality is tempered by the fact that, although all health-care professionals are to an extent managers, the large resources committed by the doctors have led to a special relationship between them and the professional managers. The fact that one profession may have more than one advisory avenue is at times regarded as privileged access whereas the real correlation with involvement in management is the extent to which a group consumes and commits resources.

It is also worth noting that while the interest of other health service staff who do not have an advisory structure is pursued through consultative machinery they are in general not recognised as having an advisory function.

Thus, although the health service is now structured to allow greater involvement of all professions and staff groups in decision-making, it is unlikely that this or any other structure will be totally satisfactory to all the groups involved. It is essential that this fact is recognised by the managers, whose responsibility it is to see that injustice or inequality of involvement is kept to a minimum. Certainly, it is unlikely to be acknowledged by those who are critical of the system in not meeting their particular expectations or advice and, understandably, it was not emphasised when the health service was reorganised. It is interesting that we are more realistic about our physical than our social environment; for example, the majority of people in this country do not really enjoy winter and, indeed, declare this very clearly – but few actually expect that the weather will be warm and sunny all year!

The problem of political expectation is one that affects more than the health service but is, perhaps, more explicit in organisations with a longer tradition and, ostensibly at least, a different ethic; but the manipulation of compromise must be done considerately as it carries a danger of alienating the essential goodwill and enthusiasm of staff. For whatever reason, in the first few years of the reorganised health service it appears that this cause of fears and uncertainties has not always been recognised by the managers themselves, a fact which has undoubtedly compounded its effects both on the staff and also on the advice which they have been prepared to offer. Thus, whatever the aim, it is undoubtedly true that professional advice from different sources has been at best fragmented and sometimes positively divisory.

External sources of advice and control

There are, of course, the two other major sources of advice to which health authorities must also respond. These are the health councils on the one hand and central government on the other. Both of these have their own peculiarities in terms of organisation but only those aspects directly relevant to the process of decision-making need to be considered here. In effect, as with the rest of the advisory structure, health councils are not directly involved in the actual decision about a particular proposal but must be informed, consulted and given the opportunity to comment on any withdrawal of services and major alteration or addition to services. Further, the health council may at any time enquire about the authority's policy or the level of provision of any particular service. The authority, for its part, although required to receive such advice, is not required to accept it; in the event of not accepting the council's advice about the withdrawal of a major facility, for example the closure of a hospital, the disagreement must be referred to the Secretary of State before a decision is taken on implementation.

The central department, while formally leaving decisions to individual authorities, none the less exerts considerable pressure for the adoption of favoured policies. Some of this is achieved by the issue of regulations particularly, for example, in matters dealing with conditions of service for staff which can markedly influence both policy and actual services. Part of the pressure is applied by seeking the intended response of boards to consultative documents and other reports touching upon their future policy or existing allocation of resources. Although in most cases the final responsibility of the Secretary of State is waived in favour of local delegated authority, none the less, because the monitor and sanction exist, the views and preferences of the central department are seldom lightly disregarded. The decision to delegate, followed by however-well-intentioned efforts to moderate possible waywardness, has resulted in an unsatisfactory state of affairs for both the Health Departments and the Health Authorities. While not a directly intended result of this more permissive central role, an incessant flood of papers outlining, defining and qualifying the options and constraints under which the authority and its staff have to operate has led to a considerable pre-emption of administrative resources and an inhibition of purposeful local planning and policy-making. More explicit central direction might actually be preferable if the price of apparent delegation is the endless stream of paper which, simply through the need to process it effectively, prevents local administrators from planning, or even managing, their various services. The results of the current proposals for greater delegation and strong local management have yet to become manifest [19].

Summary

The present organisation of the health service is a compromise between the legacies of history, current medical and social values and the requirements of technical innovation.

In addition to the formal structure there is a separate and influential network of professional and craft groupings through which all categories of staff are involved in the preliminary stages of decision-making. As well as advice from staff, the authority must also receive and give consideration to advice from the central department and health councils so that planning decisions are eventually conditioned by a wide variety of views and interests.

9

The Operation of the Service

For a structure as complex as the National Health Service to be effective it is essential to define and adhere to a delegated decision-making process appropriate to the various functional levels. Within a health authority's own domain fairly clear levels of decision-making can be identified. The first is the overview or initial broad allocation of resources between programmes of care which determines the growth or containment of particular services. The second is units and the services themselves, for example community services or various groups of hospitals, where particular components can similarly be encouraged or discouraged in attempts to achieve a balance or redistribution of resources; indeed, depending on the size of separate budgets, the process of redistribution may with advantage be further refined where parts of services within particular sectors may be identified for the augmenting or curtailing of available resources. Finally, there are the individual teams of health-care workers who by their day-to-day decisions and adoption of practices commit not only the resources immediately at their disposal but, and often unwittingly, developments for the following and subsequent years. The importance of this last component must be appreciated because there are few comparable organisations where workers have so much discretion over their method of working and their use of resources. The implications of this apparent freedom will be discussed again after the people and issues at each level have been considered.

The overview

Any decision to allocate health-care resources should make visible the means of valuing the various options and their opportunity costs. In chapter 1, the issue of consumer sovereignty was raised and reasons given why it is not possible in health care, certainly at present, to use consumers' values. However, the public as a body does delegate valuation of options to its elected representatives in both national and local government and these bodies have, traditionally, been expected to reflect consumer preferences even if informed, precise valuation is not possible. For a variety of reasons, not immediately relevant to this discussion, the administration of the health service by local government is not acceptable but effectively, although not as a result of election, a health authority acts as an intermediate level of government. The relevant functional difference is the direction of accountability: health authorities are accountable to a nationally elected body whereas local government is directly accountable to their local electors. The selection of members of health authorities by the Secretary of State from a wide range of nominations can in theory produce a number of balances in composition, and hence likely preferences, which would not so readily be achieved by conventional election.

Valuation and ranking of options, however, also require ready access to specialised information to avoid having to mount a separate inquiry for each and every resource allocation decision. The lack of hard, quantifiable data will be discussed in chapter 10; the compromise, in the meantime, must be to find individuals or groups who by virtue of their knowledge or experience are best qualified to act as substitutes. Two possible groups immediately spring to mind – the health-care managers and the health-care professionals, both of whom are represented in the decision-making structure. Health-care administrators can provide specific suggestions for the efficient use of particular resources and may be able to offer modifications of these proposals on the basis of past experience of what is likely to be acceptable; however, they, as a group, are no more qualified than any other to say what is fair for consumers as a whole. Health-care professionals on the other hand are acutely aware of the facilities and services of value to their particular patients and of help to their immediate colleagues; they can, of course, also recognise the needs of services remote to their own interests but the nature of their commitment and the purposes of their employment are to use rather than to allocate resources.

Indeed for some of this group the nature of many of the day-to-day decisions they must make explains the expectation and confidence with which they give advice, but even for the more diffident or wide-ranging health-care professionals the selection of priorities carries an inevitable and understandable bias. For these reasons the attributes of professional qualification and experience are potential disadvantages in broad policy-making.

Thus, public, patients, professionals and managers are each associated with particular biases which must inevitably influence their valuation of options. At the overview, or broad resource allocation level, choices primarily involve the value of priorities for care of the whole population; priorities which, although requiring specialised information about how best or most efficiently to achieve them, are (or should be) most concerned with the values of the community being served. The health authority therefore, has to absorb and coordinate the advice which it receives from the many formal sources referred to earlier and because they are in effect the representatives of the local community, thereafter make its own valuation of priorities for the area. It then has to endeavour to allocate resources in line with these priorities.

Although the detail may vary, most health authorities operate within a similar framework and follow an established cycle. Three sources of money are available: first, the recurrent revenue for the purpose of maintaining and developing the various services and facilities; second, non-recurrent monies used to replace equipment, maintain existing buildings and undertake both modest alterations or the construction of new buildings; and, third, the capital building programme concerned with major building works. With attempts by central government to contain public expenditure, almost inevitably health authorities have used building maintenance funds to relieve apparent short falls in service provision. In consequence the health departments have earmarked a specific maintenance allocation which may not be used for any other purpose. Some virement is possible between the remaining minor capital monies and recurrent expenditure but the sums involved are relatively small.

There also tends to be an assumption that what has been done before should go on, thereby limiting flexibility, and more questioning of this assumption is required. As a result of this lack of questioning and without redeployment being actively pursued, some 97 to 98 per cent of the recurrent revenue, in practice, is committed to maintaining the existing services and therefore the remainder (that is only 2 to 3 per cent) is expected to finance new developments, increased numbers of staff, the maintenance of new equipment and any increased cost as a result of betterment achieved through the building programme. Non-recurrent funds, averaging one-twentieth of the recurrent budget, are also available each year but care is needed in case the implications of their use carry subsequent recurrent consequences. The major building programme is organised nationally, with each area putting forward its needs which are then allocated a place in a rolling programme after comparison with, and therefore competition with, the claims from other areas. Money to meet the effects of wage awards and inflation was guaranteed by central government as were the recurrent financial consequences of major building works. These practices of inflation proofing and underwriting the running costs of new buildings have been phased out and now have to be met from either existing or development monies – yet another argument for a more flexible approach to the total recurrent budget.

Health authorities, therefore, while receiving advice from many sources, must finally balance the implications of these interacting but discrete sources of money. It is often not appreciated that, despite what may appear an enormous available sum of money, the actual amount uncommitted and thereby immediately available for developments is very small. As a result, there is a need to be increasingly looking to reductions in existing services to free some of the committed resources for alternative uses.

All developments involving medical staff and most involving nursing staff are controlled directly by the health authority and in general, although the practice will vary, schemes involving a substantial proportion of the available money, or emergencies with a threatened breakdown of a major service, will be initiated or considered by the authority. These schemes may well have been suggested at a lower level but because of the cost implications the authority itself supervises a list of such developments and periodically reviews the older priorities against the more recent additions to the list.

At unit level and within the major services

The next level is the unit but in effect these allocations are simply an aggregate of the budgets of the various services provided. At this level the health-care administrators rather than the health-care professionals are still involved. The service budgets requested for any one year are based on last year's allocations with the addition of developments that were actually funded during the previous year. Further developments are not included in these estimates and are only funded later depending on the money still left or released. As a result, change, reallocation and choice are not usually controlled at this level.

Since most of the money is already committed to maintaining the existing services and in the absence of a positive policy of redeployment, the bulk of the administrative activity at unit is directed to sustaining the status quo. The major monies available for developments are also committed because of the recurrent expenditure consequences either of higher decisions on new or strengthened services or of Government negotiations with the professions at national level. Monies available at this intermediate level come from two sources; first, from the development balances left after the major schemes have been financed and, second, usually appearing later in the year, further money either held previously in reserve or released by the central department as a result of the slippage of programmes in other areas. Not all this money is available for recurrent purposes, particularly that resulting from slippage, but by effecting a balance between the capital and recurrent needs of developments new services and improvements can be obtained. In the majority of instances the intermediate administrative levels maintain a list of desirable developments involving varying proportions of capital and recurrent implications so that relatively quick advantage may be taken of money that is made available. As most medical and nursing developments with their relatively greater cost implications are determined by the authority itself, the intermediate levels inevitably deal with other categories of staff. An exception to this would be the large infusion of money for the general improvement of a service, as has happened with geriatric and mental deficiency services, but even then increases in medical staffing (other than general practitioners) are still strictly controlled and, of course, must have the approval of the central department. Although there has always been the possibility of redeploying existing resources, with the exception of major changes in disease patterns (and hence a natural reduction in demand) it has all too seldom been used by the authorities or intermediate levels as a means of promoting developments. The most obvious opportunities have been the falling incidence of tuberculosis with the curtailment of services over a relatively short period and the more gradual reduction of services for infectious disease in general. Both events freed resources on a significant scale and allowed developments using both buildings and staff for other services. Examples of planned cut-backs to allow redeployment are, however, hard to find and yet in the future may represent the major source of such funding.

Thus, at the second level, there is at present a predominant concern with maintaining existing services and little overt acknowledgement of the values placed on these compared with new developments.

Depending upon the size of the various administrative sections, the management process may be partly repeated at a lower level, which often involves a large hospital complex or a number of small hospitals with or without the surrounding community services. The budgets may be substantial but the pattern of control, deployment and initiation is, in effect, identical to the level above through which all submissions and developments are routed. There is, however, another important function which ought to be carried out at this level. By custom, decision-making at a higher level, instead of indicating overall priorities has earmarked funds for particular developments. This has come about partly to exercise control and partly because of the demands on development monies. As a result it has been very difficult to redress previous anomalies between the allocations to individual services. What neither the authorities nor the services have ever faced up to is that the reallocation of last year's resources means that all the existing activities are, albeit unwittingly, being valued simply by being allowed to continue. They are not just valued but are implicitly valued above new development even if funded and certainly above proposed developments not yet funded.

Authorities, in theory, should have knowledge of the priorities ascribed by individual services to existing activities when reviewing the allocations and reassessing their valuations of overall priorities. As this is unlikely ever to be practical and, perhaps more fundamental, would remove from the services an important responsibility, the alternative is to create both the opportunity and incentive for such valuations and assessments to be carried out at lower levels of the structure. To a degree that could without question be increased, a modest redistribution, at present mainly by differential development authorised by the authority, takes place at the intermediate levels; but what are the possibilities of changing both allocations and use at the level of the health-care team or individual practitioner?

Individual services or health-care teams

The final level at which the care and various support services operate varies considerably in management and organisation depending in the main on the type of staff and the nature of the service. The demands and the responsibilities vary and there are three relatively distinct contexts in which the methods and problems of meeting the demand can usefully be examined. The first is the *basic support services* – catering, cleaning, heating and so on (the so-called 'hotel' services). Here, demand is largely predictable and levels of output or norms have been calculated (such as the costs of cleaning or heating a given area or the costs per 100 meals). Budgets are clearly known. A high level of control is therefore possible and the results of change, in terms of staff or methods of working, are predictable.

With the second, *para-clinical*, services – perhaps best exemplified by a laboratory – although the trend in demand for existing examinations can be predicted the overall total or demand for an individual test is less certain. Control can partly be maintained by more efficient techniques. Here again budgets are known, control is still possible but is not entirely in the hands of the head of department and therefore the results of change in policy or practice are far less certain.

Third, in the *clinical* field, because of the much smaller size and varied composition of the working teams, the resources available to the individual health worker are not known except in the most general terms; the aim is to meet overt demand, and the methods of meeting these demands are not only extremely varied but continually changing. It is possible, for example, for a surgeon to introduce a new operating techniques which has profound implications for nurses and anaesthetists and by offering what may amount to a new service create a large demand from general practitioners on behalf of patients previously unknown to the hospital service. Budgets, therefore, are not fully appreciated, control has no clear context and the extent, let alone the effect, of change is also unknown. There are two other relevant factors; the first is that although the various health care and supporting workers form a work team the individual members have been drawn from a number of discrete functional services, each with its own management structure and separate budget. Vigorous attempts are now being made to introduce more realistic budgeting procedures [69]. Inevitably the management of the resource provided by the team and the management of the resources represented by the basic functional units are at times in conflict. The second and related factor is the growth of health care professions. An interesting example of this trend can be found in the changed attitudes and expectations of domestic staff which have given rise to the concept of housekeeping teams to provide bedmaking and similar services peripatetically as opposed to the previous arrangement of a maid attached to a single ward. The development of domestic services in this way, with a recognised training programme, certification and a separate line management structure, presents the health service with yet another manifestation of the specialist dilemma. There is no denying the potential value of a specialised approach but there is a danger of continuing fragmentation of the care given to the patients. How far should specialisation go and where does the balance lie? The breaking up into defined components of care makes redeployment and changed methods of working much more difficult to introduce; this loss of flexibility is in no sense the root of the problem but its coincident emergence is an added complication that must be recognised. The significance of these developments at this final level of decision-making can not be emphasised too strongly because it creates a situation in which leadership and goals are divided and different.

Thus at the level of individual services or health-care teams the question of control is of prime importance. At one extreme there can be clear line management structure with a single manager who knows the budget and resources available to the department and who controls and manipulates these to meet as far as possible the various demands made upon that part of the service. Examples are portering, cleaning and perhaps maintenance. In these instances the demands, while by no means finite, can largely be anticipated and manipulated.

Between the extremes are the para-clinical or supporting services such as the clinical laboratories, investigatory departments (for example, X-ray), the various therapy departments (for example, physiotherapy) and the supply departments (for example, pharmacy). In these instances a form of line management exists with, most often, a departmental head or specialist in administrative charge. Budgets either as a sum of money or as resources such as staff and equipment are known and the services must be provided within them. If demand exceeds supply it is usually regulated by a waiting time for particular items of service and access is determined by a system of priority categories. An exception is pharmacy, which attempts to meet virtually all demands; the cost implications, however, are regularly monitored and if a large over-spending appears likely either additional funds are allocated or a general request for a review of prescribing is sent to the clinical departments. At the other extreme are the senior medical staff with no line structure whatsoever. By the nature of their specialty some of these health care professionals are able to operate alone and use such facilities as they deem necessary for the care of the patients referred to them. This method of working is the exception rather than the rule but since it exists, certainly in practice if not actually within the organisational description, it has to be accommodated. Such individuals admit patients to beds, arrange out-patient sessions, order laboratory investigations and nursing treatments, require the time of junior medical staff and utilise secretarial services and in this way commit the services of other people and departments. Demands from these individuals are uncoordinated with those of their colleagues and thereby are less amenable to manipulation by the other managers. Even when the health-care professionals operate as a team the very nature of their work means that their demands for resources are similar to those of staff working independently. The difference, however, is that other departments in trying to meet these requests for services find it easier to negotiate with a team, who, in turn, can then co-ordinate and modify their methods of working. Similar teams also join to form a division or specialty group and finally the various groups come together as a comprehensive hospital or specialist medical staff committee. The precise arrangements vary from one part of the country to another but, in general, this body also nominates a proportion of the members of the medical advisory committee and thus the communication on the medical specialist side is usually complete. Unlike the para-clinical services, the clinical units have no line management or consultant in administrative charge but most teams work through an annually elected chairman. The clinical teams, also, have no budget and individual specialists order the various services required by their patients. There are, however, certain restraints in that resources such as operating theatres, anaesthetists and out-patient clinics are finite and therefore must be shared on some agreed basis. Similarly, individual services such as physiotherapy or particular radiological investigations may be in short supply and therefore patients requiring these may have to wait. Equipment may be requested but not actually ordered by an individual specialist and thus a measure of financial control is possible. It would undoubtedly be more effective if the clinicians directly controlled their budgets [69]. Not only would this provide greater control it would make clinicians more aware of the rest of the resources they were using; the reasons why this does not happen are largely historical. When the health service started there was genuine concern that the quality of care available to patients would be unduly determined by financial considerations and that therefore, above all, the 'clinical freedom' of clinicians had to be assured. For this reason, the provision of budgets for clinical services was deemed inappropriate and the accounting system devised for purposes of audit made it extremely difficult to relate the costs of resources used to the care of individual patients. Despite this, partial financial control was achieved by creating budgets for the para-clinical services and by general constraints on some of the major identifiable resources used by the clinical service. In the face of these limitations on control it is to the credit of the health service administrators and staff that costs have been kept remarkably close to the financial allocations.

Pre-emption of resources

One other major activity requires special consideration, namely staff training. The issues involved are well demonstrated in the case of nursing. Numerically it is one of the largest groups within the health service. It is organised within a clear hierarchical structure and is contained by a separate and predetermined budget. Within this overall nursing total, sub-budgets are allocated to various functional divisions (for example, general, domiciliary, paediatric, psychiatric, maternity) and the nursing establishments so created are one of the major constraints in the development or modification of services. Funds allocated to nursing may not be used for other purposes without the approval of the health authority and both the size and ubiquitous nature of this particular part of the total budget carries important implications for management and planning. There are, however, other aspects that are not solely at the discretion of the health authority, particularly nurse training and recruitment [53]. The need for adequate standards in both training and staffing is undeniable but it is unfortunate that the price of this safeguard is yet another form of national norm which is then less sensitive and responsive to local circumstances.

Because the numbers entering nurse training are geared to existing levels of trained staff it is extremely difficult once a shortage has occurred ever to recover unless qualified nurses can be recruited from outside an area. In this way a severe restriction to an essential resource not only is imposed but also is completely outside the control of the authority. Obviously, it is no solution to erode the standards of training but the consequence is that consideration may have to be given either to a redefinition of tasks or to an acceptance that particular forms of care can no longer be provided, with all the implications that such a decision would entail.

These training issues go further in the pre-emption of an authority's resources. The health service trains a large proportion of staff and the standards are supervised, as already mentioned, by a variety of independent professional organisations. Not only do these organisations assess the competence of the trainees but they also stipulate the precise training schedules and the required staffing, accommodation and facilities that must be provided before such training programmes are recognised and approved.

There is much to commend the approach but it must also be appreciated that this is merely another forum in which competition for resources is taking place. Within the service itself groups must make a case for resources which is then judged against other priorities; in this instance the case is a requirement which if not met prohibits the training activity. The extent to which these arrangements allow more pressing priorities to be over-ridden and, indeed, the extent to which these self same groups are, unwittingly, making decisions in one capacity which then deprive them of resources they desperately need in another, are matters that have to be examined if a proper balance and an equitable distribution of resources are to be achieved.

This problem is not confined to the clinical services. Similar dilemmas exist within the Ambulance Service, where again the need for national standards in crew numbers and training levels for accident and emergency work is distorting the requirements for providing the complementary, non-emergency local transport facilities. These issues range beyond a straightforward statement of health care needs into the more complex negotiations of employment opportunity and pay differentials. The distinction between the different forms that resources available to the health service can take, namely money, manpower and materials, may appear academic since a shortage in the latter two could be solved simply by an increase in the former. None the less the distinction is important, certainly in the short term, because if there is a shortage of trained staff and appropriate buildings or equipment then some people or patients must make do with a lower quality of care or perhaps go without. If this is not satisfactory, it must be appreciated that more money alone will not immediately, or even in the foreseeable future, solve the shortfall because buildings and training programmes can take upwards of a decade to become functional or to create more trained staff. To overcome this time lag will require the use of less-skilled personnel and here other problems arise: if the less skilled are paid at the standard rate what is the point of undergoing training? If, however, they are paid less then the job is being undervalued and the skill diluted.

There are, in fact, three issues that must be recognised and reconciled. First, the possibility that the health service is over-training staff in relation to the actual tasks that have to be performed. If it is quite unacceptable to the current ethos of society that skill differentials should be expressed as wide financial differences then it will be very difficult in overcoming specific manpower shortages to meet health-care needs by employing untrained staff. However, the primary object of employing less-skilled people would not be to save money but to provide some sort of service rather than none at all and some means must be found to restore at least a measure of flexibility and a better return for the resources used. Second, it may be that dilution of skills is more dangerous than a reduction of volume of service, in which case far more consideration will have to be given to assessing priorities for care. Third, and most important, given the need to operate within these competing factors and in the face of the skill implications of technology in health care it follows that there will never be an end to the demand for resources and the need to make choices. The health-care professions and the public must acknowledge these facts and appreciate that every improvement in staff conditions of work and training standards, however apt, has itself an opportunity cost and that it is not possible to divorce these from the requirements for health care as all are making demands upon the same finite resource. There is no separate fund to deal with problems which may appear peripheral to health care; health-care planning must therefore take account of all these diverse pressures in devising the appropriate services.

Summary

Because of the complexities and conflicts in terms of priority choices of individuals and state in the provision of health care, some form of agency relationship is inevitable. As public, patients and professionals are to an extent barred, a group, selected and constituted as a health authority have been given this responsibility. In addition to being viewed with some suspicion health authorities currently lack the hard data upon which to base decisions and must therefore attempt to absorb and value the advice and options they receive from many sources.

Approaches which suit one part of the service may carry considerable implications, indeed complications, for another and perhaps the most important but often forgotten implications are the diverse demands made unwittingly on the same finite resource.

Too often both public and health service staff are unaware that demands although not arising directly from health-care needs must nevertheless compete with and possibly displace pressing clinical priorities.

10
Planning and Health Care

In the first section of this book, an attempt was made to show how the philosophy and techniques of economics could assist planning and decision making in health care. In chapter 9 the operation of the service was described in terms of levels of decision-making, financial control, advice and consultation. The omission of any description of a planning and evaluation framework reflects the reality of the current process of resource allocation within authorities despite the developing planning cycle, at least in England, which is intended to revolve around detailed patient-orientated plans produced at the operational level. In this chapter, the absence of a planning framework is discussed and a proposal made for a more efficient structure which would allow health service staff to focus on the aspects of planning and evaluation appropriate to their varying levels of responsibility.

Before reorganisation, there was a gradual development of the concept of planning – in the sense of looking ahead to estimate or decide how future services might be improved – but it was applied only disjointedly to discrete components of health services such as hospital beds and manpower and, apart from minor capital schemes, mainly at national level. Quite separately, forecasts were made of revenue expenditure and the growth rates which would be required to provide certain services but no framework was created within which separate resource inputs could be costed, amalgamated and set against expected outputs. The need to change the focus of planning from services or inputs to patients or outputs was explicitly stated in the discussions before reorganisation (see, for example, the 'Grey' book [13]) and a comprehensive planning structure was proposed, based on client or patient-orientated programmes of care. Subsequently, and particularly in England, considerable effort at national level went into promoting a planning cycle in which strategic plans (that is, long-term 'directional' policy) were created at regional level and compatible operational plans were devised, implemented and monitored at area and district. In this way it was intended to ensure that broad national (and regional) policy guidelines are followed but that the choice of the actual deployment of resources from year to year was delegated to districts and geared to the priorities and expected benefits for particular populations as identified by the patient- or client-care professionals.

In the 1982 reorganisation the district has become the basic planning body with a shorter rolling programme and attempts to reduce variations between localities by monitoring specific performance indicators [19].

In the face of these obvious efforts to introduce rational, output-orientated planning into the health service it may seem unfair to criticise the system which is now evolving. However, it is precisely because there is a search for better planning approaches that the authors of this book believe that it is timely to offer some constructive criticism and, it is hoped, useful alternatives.

Relating outputs to inputs

The first point is that, although the cycle allows for a greater consideration of outputs, the relationship of inputs to outputs remains disjointed. Indeed, it is implicit in the planning cycle that the definition of desirable outputs and benefits should precede the consideration of costs. The remit of the health-care planning teams (or programme committees) is to produce policy recommendations and optional plans which *thereafter* are costed; the selection of how to distribute the available resources is then made by a different body. Thus the cost of composite packages can be compared but there is no point at which the possible benefits of alternative uses of specific resources can be clearly evaluated – in other words, the opportunity costs cannot be spelt out. Even if a single group both devised plans and also had control of the allocation of resources, the fact that outputs and inputs are not considered simultaneously decreases the likelihood that realistic alternatives and opportunity costs are considered. Hence the best choice of options, in terms of obtaining the maximum benefit from the limited allocations, is less likely to be made.

Information for planning

The second, and related, point is that there has been no change in the information available for making choices. There is a tendency to think that because a planning system has been created choices will be more rational and objective. This is not so. Information consists of both values and data. The conflicts of values at all levels of the health service are an integral part of its design and it is essential that members and officers understand the nature of these conflicts so that the work of the various groups is directed to what is commonly possible rather than what is individually desirable. There is in fact a danger that the need to produce detailed plans, particularly at the multiprofessional programme level, will divert attention away from discussion of values and will concentrate the activities of the group on data-gathering as a substitute for, rather than as a complement to, evaluation. This danger arises just as much, if not more, in multi-agency or 'joint' planning. At the operational level, for example in the care of the elderly, there is an obvious need for joint policies and co-ordination of plans and services between local authorities and health services. The additional issue of conflict in joint planning groups is how these bodies can be a common source of multiprofessional advice about priorities and possibilities in care without inhibiting their other planning activities. One of the difficulties of inter-agency co-ordination is that the organisational financial structures differ in line with the separate origins and functions of the agencies concerned. A key to this dilemma may lie in shared funding (termed 'joint financing' in England and 'support financing' in Scotland). It is perhaps too soon to judge whether health and local government agencies will be able to make imaginative use of the joint finance but it does appear so far that the inclusion of a time-limit after which joint schemes must be wholly financed by local government is hindering the evolution of a truly joint approach to planning. The recent extension of the time-limit may encourage local government but has also increased anxieties within the acute services that funds that might have been available for more direct health purposes are being pre-empted. The separation which Boddy [2] makes between the role of officers in setting out alternative plans and the role of members (in his instance, of programme committees) in valuing these alternatives is fundamental to an efficient planning system, whether it be within health or between health and other agencies. It is the same separation outlined in the earlier chapters of this book; it not only allows the members to see that their role *is* to apply values it also makes proper use of the skills and training of officers in preparing plans rather than, as may happen, merely keeping minutes and arranging the dates of the next meeting. This, in turn, distinguishes the needs of officers for training in the preparation of alternative plans from those of members for guidance in asking the right questions.

The lack of information about the effectiveness of care for many options in health-care planning has led to efforts being concentrated on improving the ways in which other types of information may be handled and translated into 'intelligence'. The three main types of numerical data which are included describe the population, its epidemiological characteristics and health-care resources, including utilisation or 'activity' data. However, while health information systems have become more sophisticated they do not yet routinely provide information in a framework geared to the planning choices which have to be made – and remade. As already indicated, following the Körner Steering Group recommendations a determined and substantial effort is being made to improve the information available [21, 61] but almost inevitably the data still relate to inputs rather than outputs. The need to present inputs alongside outputs has already been stated and the use of programme budgeting is a step in this direction, with sub-programme structures being of particular relevance in devising operational plans. The purpose of programme budgeting is to describe the resource use by each programme or sub-programme set against whatever measures of output are available, as a first step towards making judgements about priorities. The use of comparisons or relatives is perhaps the most usual substitute for hard information about outputs when setting priorities or targets; indeed, it is so common a practice that many who use it have forgotten – or, if they are new to the game have never realised – that irrelevant comparisons can lead to irrelevant conclusions. It is therefore worth commenting on the relevance to local planning of the factors that are most frequently used to judge the relative priorities of particular areas, services or programmes. They are used on the basis either of the gap between the actual supply and a desirable norm or target or of the level locally compared with other areas or the national average.

Perhaps most frequently used, when it exists, is the national 'norm' *per capita* for a particular resource such as types of hospital bed or manpower. Judgements have been made, both nationally and locally, that priority should be given to those areas or services which are furthest below the national norm. However, it is important to recognise the purpose and origins of such figures. When they first appeared in the Hospital Plans for England [43] and Scotland [23] they were presented as desirable rates of provision to improve the services given by certain specialties but ones which, it was anticipated, should not have to be exceeded except in very unusual circumstances.

Since then, norms of supply have appeared for other hospital specialties, for some facilities outside hospital and for some types of staff but they do not exist for all types of resources. Those which have been produced have been based on discrete studies or working party reports and usually have contained elements of both 'good practice' and expert opinion. Unfortunately, the variables, included in the estimates have seldom been spelt out and there is, therefore, no way of knowing how they might be affected by for example changes in population or alternative patterns of care. In 1978, the Department of Health and Social Security circulated to all English health authorities a useful critique [14] of the use of norms and indicators for manpower planning in which they underlined the dangers of applying them locally without knowledge of their inherent assumptions and the same caveats apply to norms for other resources. In addition, there has never been any pretence that an efficient balance of care *between* services was being proposed, nor has there been any explicit recognition of the resource consequences of trying to attain one or more of them. The continuation of the use of 'norms', at least for the next few years, is clearly seen in the recommendations of the new Scottish Capital Building Programme and the proposals give little encouragement to planners wishing to develop a more flexible and more rational approach, based on a weighing up of the relevant costs and benefits of alternative courses of action [60].

Thus, norms of supply are of little value within health areas in helping to select priorities between or within programmes. Obviously, to aim for a national norm for, say, surgical beds in all districts is a move to equality of supply of that one service (which may or may not be a desirable objective depending on the extent to which needs vary) but it does not help at all in placing a priority on achieving that level of surgical beds *vis-à-vis* some level of another service for which there is no norm. Unfortunately, however, because norms have been for a long time one of the few quantified targets in existence they have become absorbed into the everyday planning language for those programmes or services for which they have been created nationally. The phrase 'we should have *x* psychiatric beds per 1000 population' is all too often heard as the final and irrefutable argument for additional resources for this facility and the best *balance* of services is never considered because there are no norms for alternative patterns of care within the psychiatric programme, and no consideration given to attempting to compare the benefits of a number of psychiatric beds with those of, say, an anti-smoking campaign.

The assumption that the aim of geographical equality of supply is a sufficient basis for allocating resources between programmes also underlies the widespread use of comparison of local supply with that in other areas and districts or with the national *average* rates of supply (which may be very different from the norm). It is common practice to rank the health districts in order of level of provision of services and to judge from that which local services should take priority for expansion. Utilisation rates such as 'beds used per 1000 population' are often similarly compared. Given the variation which exists across Britain in density, age-structure and occupation of populations, to aim for national averages in all areas ignores the fact that needs vary between areas.

There is another type of norm or rate which is also used comparatively, when it exists, as an argument for changing relative priorities for services and that is the professionally-determined level of provision, of facilities or manpower, to meet desirable standards of care or practice. Target levels of nurse staffing, of laboratory services or of equipment are widely used in judging whether claim A or claim B should be supported – and used without due consideration of the costs of meeting these target levels. Often the aims of improved working conditions, job satisfaction or efficiency are clearly stated and, despite the absence of cost data, may well be judged to be sufficient justification for an increased allocation. However, sometimes there is an implication or assumption, in this as in the other types of comparisons, that proportionate or even greater benefit will ensue to the health of the local population. The drawback of all three sets of data should be clear: they are geared solely to inputs, rather than to both inputs and outputs. For a health authority they are not costly to obtain (if they have been produced nationally) and each does have a use. National norms, although not intended for application within health areas as desirable standards of care to meet local needs, do let authorities know that any claims for resources to exceed the stated rate can only be met by giving up another local resource and even then will require cogent arguments to obtain national sanction. National averages or inter-area comparisons enable an authority to identify an area comparable in population and perhaps needs and make a more detailed comparison of the nature of inputs and outputs in the two areas. Professionally-determined rates of supply also help to focus on aspects of services which may require closer investigation. None, however, should alone (or even in combination) influence local priorities because they are all aimed at equality of supply or use rather than at trying to ensure the more efficient and effective use of the resources available to provide the maximum amount of health for the people in the area.

The other two types of numerical information mentioned earlier are based on epidemiological and population data.

Epidemiological data about a population are usually used for planning by applying to them criteria of care and so deriving estimates of need for care according to currently desirable standards. The arguments against the use of comprehensive epidemiological surveys which are translated into estimates of 'met' and 'unmet' need have been presented in chapters 3 and 6 and marginal analysis offered as a more relevant and, indeed, quicker and cheaper technique which defines not only the characteristics of those people and services most likely to be affected by a shift in resources but also relates the characteristics of those affected to the resources which are involved in their care.

Population data introduce a slightly different but related comment which highlights what are perhaps the main criticisms of the current use of information systems for planning (other than the lack of measures of effectiveness or benefit). These are, first, the failure to look ahead; second, the lack of awareness that uncertainty can be reduced; and third, the failure to relate the different types of data to each other in a way which is relevant to planning and evaluation questions and choices. It is axiomatic that planning means looking ahead and yet the use of projections in planning is a remarkably recent phenomenon. Perhaps the classic example is the lack of anticipation of the impact of the elderly population explosion; even although the population projections were available, few if any plans were considered for adapting services in advance. One possible explanation is the uncertainty of population predictions because of unforeseen fluctuations in such variables as birth rates and migration (although the elderly are the group least likely to be subject to such uncertainty); however, a more likely explanation is that, although the predictions were accepted, the implications for services were just too big to be tackled by health-care planners who had no real power to shift resources.

Patterns of disease and technology are also difficult to predict, as are factors which may influence the availability of resources. Despite all these uncertainties it is still feasible, and desirable, by the use of sensitivity analysis to forecast the different effects of a realistic range of possible developments. 'Scenarios' which show the implication of certain trends or policies are vital in setting limits to the options that are actually available. In chapter 2 an example was given of extrapolations of programme expenditure and similar extrapolations or projections for manpower, for populations or for disease groups can help the planner to focus on possible future demands as well as resources. The danger is that only one plan or package is devised. In coping with uncertainty it is essential to be aware of the need to check regularly which scenario is likely to be nearest reality and whether a change of policy is required. If the possible alternatives have been recognised in advance, the planners are prepared for change and have therefore a greater degree of flexibility and capacity to adapt. The choice of variables and the way in which they may behave depends on expert knowledge and accurate information and, once again, the danger for the planner or manager is in not taking a sufficiently wide view of alternatives.

Incentives for planning

There is a barrier to effective planning within the present organisation of the health service. Within boards, authorities, programme committees, health-care planning teams, geographically or functionally discrete services, or large departments which are allocated distinct budgets a degree of comparison of outputs with inputs is possible, even if not synchronised; however, those who work as part of teams or as sub-groups within a larger service not only lack the information but also are unlikely to be so motivated because reassessment of existing practices is unlikely to free identifiable resources which could then be made available to the individuals who initiate the changes. The question of incentives is fundamental. Considerable emphasis has already been placed on the need to distinguish clearly between the two levels at which decisions are made. At one level broad priorities are laid down which in turn clearly indicate the direction of the medium and long-term developments. At the next level a further set of more specific priorities is then decided within these guidelines for the short and medium term. The two are separate, require different skills or experience and although not totally discrete should normally be carried out by different groups of people. The important issue for both groups, however, is that once they have received the guidelines from the level above they are free to manage and manipulate their resources against the priorities they themselves have set and with which, therefore, they can clearly identify. Without these incentives it is difficult to introduce or sustain the application of economic techniques at the very level of health service operation where the majority of resources are used, namely the clinical units. It is, therefore, important to see whether or not the required opportunities or incentives can be offered. A number of issues require to be considered. The first is to find some practical means of allowing or requiring the main users of resources to identify with and work towards the goals set for their own services. At present the system favours a maintenance of what exists and, while not totally inhibiting, certainly reduces the incentive and opportunity for change.

The second is to overcome the growth of individual professional and task-based groups so that health-care teams with an identifiable budget can be formed [70]. While an aim may have been to allow greater participation in the running of services, the structure that has been evolved is driving staff into isolated, inward-looking groups whose contacts with and understanding of each other are minimal. It is ironic that people who form multidisciplinary teams when caring for patients then reform themselves into professional groups with no direct working relationships to the actual services upon which they are giving advice.

Third, the extremely cumbersome machinery of consultation now requires a disproportionate time both in the health authority and the various advisory bodies to administer the prescribed procedures. More important, as things stand, priorities and proposals by one advisory group are not seen or commented upon by others before they have reached the health board whereupon the whole process must be reversed and a further round of consultations has to be initiated. It is little wonder that, as was found during an extensive review of the services of one Scottish health board [31], there is delay, misunderstanding and frustration.

Although the frustration within the service is fairly general the key roles in resource allocation of staff working with patients make it the prime area in which to look at the scope for change but it is unlikely that a rearrangement of the existing clinical or supporting services would be acceptable or even advisable. These services would, therefore, appear to be the fixed points from which to start.

The concept of programmes of care as a means of encouraging output orientation remains attractive. The factors that would have to change are resource allocation, financial control, management, advice and consultation. The simplest suggestion would be to base each of these functions entirely within the individual services so that in terms of organisation they are near self sufficiency. This already occurs, for example in terms of management and financial control in particular sectors that are geographically distinct or in terms of resource allocation and consultative procedures in services that are discrete, such as mental deficiency services. One possibility would be to extend this facility generally and make individual units, or homogeneous parts of large units, responsible for their own budgets and for offering professional advice. This principle could be refined so that each unit would be based on specific clinical or discrete services such as child health, acute services, maternity, the elderly, the mentally ill and so on – in effect, 'programmes'. However, problems arise with certain paramedical, scientific and support services such as physiotherapy, laboratories or laundry. It would be necessary to continue locating staff in particular clinical services, as at present, when the support service maintains an overall co-ordinating function but instead of being zero-priced at the point of consumption they would, in respect of budgets, be 'purchased' by the various clinical services. Clinical service programmes would be the key to the system and would be similar to the present health-care planning teams and programme planning committees except that they would additionally be responsible for the allocation, management and budgetary control of all the resources relevant to their service. In effect each programme, or even sub-programme in the case of large acute services, would determine what they did with the resources allocated to them. The question of financial control would require particular consideration although the detail may be more appropriately a matter for an individual authority or board. Suffice it to say at this stage that the various aspects of financial control are such as to require both programme and a higher level of responsibility. At least seven or more service and programme committees would be required to represent all the various functional groups and examples of their possible composition and relationships are shown in Table 10.1. Members of the committees should come from three sources – the health-care professionals, officers and the public. Involving the public in the planning and provision of individual services would overcome a number of the claimed disadvantages of health councils. In the case of support services lay representation might not be considered necessary but a committee representing the various users would be required for the management of these services.

Under these proposals some of the existing administrative organisation would be redundant because of the delegation of a number of functions to the realigned service programmes. Generally, the staff concerned would not be changing what they do but rather the place where they do it; in this way the wasteful and frustrating feature of remote offices would be reduced. Indeed, with a large measure of delegation, the co-ordination and management functions could be carried out by lay staff located within a programme or service. The idea of many more existing central co-ordinating functions becoming a responsibility of nominated programme staff involved in the routine services is one that deserves careful consideration.

If many aspects of resource allocation, management, financial control and advisory functions were passed to units or service programmes, then 192 health districts in England and 15 health

TABLE 10.1   *Programmes and services*

Clinical programmes
   Child health
   Mental health
   Acute services*
   Geriatric services
   Primary care services†
      Medical
      Dental
      Pharmaceutical
      Ophthalmic
   Maternity services

Support services
   Paramedical·services ≠
   Scientific services
   Support services §
      Maintenance
      Catering
      Laundries, etc.

---

* Because of the size of this budget it might more appropriately be subdivided into two or three committees (for example, accident and emergency and medical and surgical services)

† The budgeting implications of practitioner services are only partly an authority responsibility and these might most effectively be considered together

≠ The dispersal of the staff in these services budgets would be conditional on other developments and therefore might be processed by a single committee

§ Because of the range and diversity of these services a number of distinct budgets may be necessary but those should be limited and coordinated by a single committee

boards in Scotland are too many. More appropriate figures would be perhaps about 60 in England and three or four in Scotland. A reduction in the number of districts and boards would have the major advantage of creating new larger areas of a size appropriate for planning; second, these new groupings could concentrate their efforts on the allocation of resources between the various programmes and on monitoring and reporting back to the individual programme committees upon the services that were being provided. The reduced number of districts under this arrangement would become the next administrative level at which the co-ordinating functions and limited management responsibilities already referred to would be carried out (see Figures 10.1 and

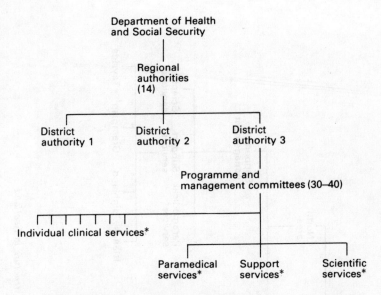

*with appropriate subdivisions and responsibilites as in Figure 10.2

FIGURE 10.1   *Outline of the proposed structure in England*

10.2). Such a brief outline inevitably dismisses points of detail but
the principles are of greater import. For example, by this means
each of the new larger districts would have about seven or eight
separate types of programme within each of the old health
authority or board areas but, more important, they would have
perhaps four or five independent programmes in the same special-
ity – for example, child health – under this supervision (see Figure
10.2). As a result each new district would in total be responsible
for between 30 and 40 programmes. This would allow for more
purposeful planning and resource allocation in that the new health
board's concern would be concentrated on comparison of resource
allocations and monitoring of outputs between, say, their five
child-health programmes. The considerations of inputs and outcomes within various sets of similar budgets provides the scope for
planning and purposeful changes in resource allocation. Similarly
the monitoring of the service programmes and the production of

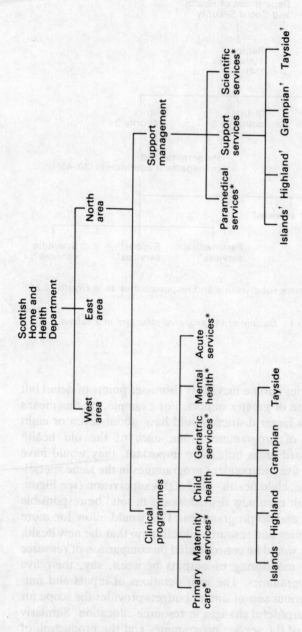

FIGURE 10.2 Outline of the proposed structure in Scotland

* with further subdivisions as appropriate
† co-ordination of services operating within programmes

reports similar in form (though obviously more extensive in content) to the Hospital Advisory Service would lead to constructive discussions and exchange of advice between the district authority or board members and the staff actually providing the services. In this way monitoring, discussion, planning and resource allocation would evolve into an effective cycle.

At the service programme level similar direct advantages accrue. First and most important, those providing the services would be able to determine their own priorities and manipulate their resources directly towards these goals. There would be no need to seek permission for reallocation as financial accountability would be vested in the programme committee and administered by the programme's own finance staff. Second, and equally important, the price of such delegated authority would be the responsibility to justify to area how and with what effect the budget was spent by answering comments or criticisms in the regular monitoring report and by comparison with other similar service programmes. These discussions could replace the present system of advisory consultations and would also form the basis of subsequent submissions for development support. There is no doubt that this proposal would require the present professional and consultative structure to be modified but this must be set against the need to relate these activities directly at a practical level to the effects on patients and patient care.

At this point it is worth returning to the suggestion of introducing lay members into this new service programme organisation. In some instances existing programme planning committees and health-care planning teams already involve with advantage health board or health authority members, representatives of services and organisations outside the health service, and, occasionally, members of health councils. This suggestion is not merely a result of nostalgia for the old boards of management and hospital management committees of the pre-1974 days but a recognition of the need to involve appropriate representatives of all the parties concerned close to the level at which the services are actually provided. Public involvement through health councils has not fully achieved the participation hoped for and many staff with experience of the previous boards of management regret their loss of contact with knowledgeable local lay members. How involvement might be achieved is open to debate but the presence of another group representing the patients when the decisions are made on how to use the resources allocated to a programme is essential. Lay members of the programme committees would also compensate for the reduction in total health board and district health authority members and could take a share in serving on the various appeals and professional committees required by statute.

This approach goes a long way towards reducing the disadvantages of the present system particularly in respect of effective planning and yet maintains the aim of greater staff and public participation and, at the very least, simplifies the structure of the service.

The staff providing the individual services and the patients receiving them to a large extent would be setting their own goals and any change or saving in their use of resources would leave that resource immediately available to them to use against their other priorities. District or area would determine the size of an individual programme budget but how that budget was subsequently spent would be a matter for the programme committee. Second, the multidisciplinary team providing the care would be the same team who also determined the deployment and management of their resources. Third, it would be again the same team proferring advice to district and area and discussing the need for improvements and developments. To argue that breaking down into discrete service programmes, as suggested, acts against the concept of integration would not be valid because this was not the form of division that has in any way been affected by integration. Indeed, a previous form of integration would be regained in that the change in emphasis from district to programmes would mean a movement back for administrators, managers and finance officers into closer day-to-day contact and working relationships with their health care colleagues and the public.

Summary

Planners are becoming more aware of the need for reliable information on which to base their selection of priorities, particularly for operational plans. However, they seem less aware of the need for planning techniques and the decision-making aids such as those outlined in the early chapters of this book. No planning technique can provide objective measures of benefit across the range of programmes provided by a health authority; nor should it be expected to do so. However, three important components of planning are underused. These are

(1) the devising and costing of alternative plans and, in particular, *simultaneous* consideration of costs and benefits for different options;
(2) the use of projections or broad scenarios to increase awareness of possible future changes in policy variables; and
(3) the creation of a framework or a set of frameworks within which planning and priorities should take place and which is related to the decisions to be taken at each level of planning.

There is an obvious distinction in purpose and content between strategic and operational plans, a varying emphasis on consumer and professional values according to the level of decision-making and a decreasing availability of comparable, final outcome measures as choices shift from disease or problem-specific uses of resources and outputs towards the selection of priorities from a heterogeneous range of services or programmes. Unfortunately, information designed for one level tends to be used at other levels simply because it exists and despite the fact that it does not answer the questions which should be asked at these other levels. Indeed, by being used inappropriately it actively prompts the wrong questions and thus leads to confusion about planning roles and failure to devise coherent and comprehensive plans which can be implemented and monitored. A framework is urgently required against which the nature of the choices to be made at each level becomes apparent and which assists in determining what information is relevant to these choices.

Determining choices, however, is only one part of the problem and there remains the need to find some way by which staff are able to identify with the priorities established for their services. In this respect the present structure is inhibiting and is drawing staff into isolated groups with few opportunities to identify with the goals of their local services and too many frustrations from cumbersome consultative machinery. It is suggested that the number of health boards and authorities be reduced, that districts should be removed and that the structure should be based on redefined clinical services. These services should be managed by groups drawn from the professions, officers and the public and should incorporate the advisory structure and health councils. Local services would determine their own priorities and manipulate their resources and the price of such delegated authority would be an annual comparison with other similar local service programmes.

While the techniques and approaches of economists, even strengthened by changes in the structure, cannot solve all the problems which health-care planners face they can go a long way to assist them in their tasks.

11

Some of the Choices

This book has dealt with the opportunities for application of economic techniques to health-care planning. Few would doubt the logic of the philosophy underlying the work which has been described; resources are and always will be scarce and the public, patients, professionals and planners all have an interest in seeing that the resources which do exist are used to the best effect. Rather more people would question whether the choices which are made reflect the 'proper' value of what is best; it would be naive and misleading to ignore the fact that there are almost as many ideas of what is best at any one time as there are people interested in health care. In the market-place of private medicine it is possible, and appropriate, for each consumer to choose the best use of his own resources according to his values at that time. The opportunity cost in the balance is the alternative use of his own money and the alternative benefits from the other uses of the medical resources is irrelevant. However, in a community system the emphasis shifts; the consumer can no longer buy just what he wants and the responsibility for weighing up the alternative uses of his and everyone else's money lies with the government and its representatives or nominees at local level. Because the choices of which services to provide and which not to provide are taken on his behalf, however indirectly, the consumer has a right to have the opportunity to know the bases on which they are made. Therefore there is a responsibility on health authorities to let their public know when, say, one service is expanding or another contracting and the reasons for the shifts in emphasis, whether planned or haphazard. Clearly, to do so the health authorities must themselves know both the extent of the change that is occurring and, also, why. The issue of whether or not it is possible to reach a consensus of values shared by the health services and

157

the local consumers is not directly part of this argument; the point is that the relative values applied by the health services should, by rights, be made explicit to the people who are paying for them. The relevance of the difficulty of consensus is that it creates confusion in the minds of too many people about the different types of decisions that have to be made and, more important, about the nature of their contribution to the decision-making. Perhaps the critical component in the functioning of the service is the means by which people actually participate and it is likely that many of the problems at present facing the health service stem from attempts to introduce yet further managerial change. It is all too easy to criticise and to exaggerate defects but the problem for the health service, and for that matter any modern society, is the need to balance general with expert opinion and to recognise the separate processes determining social judgement and technical judgements. Within the health service the means of obtaining, assessing and acting upon the general and expert view have become hopelessly entangled. To argue that such confusion is the source of much of the health service's ills may seem facile but the need to avoid professionalism and special pleading is as much a matter of concern today as it was before attempts were made to make the service more democratic. There is a real danger that the application of the principle of greater participation, instead of rectifying the situation, has merely strengthened the power and increased the number of pressure groups. Social and expert groups will inevitably and understandably promote the activities with which they are associated. What is necessary is that these perfectly proper demands are seen in context.

At the present time too many of the decisions, and arguments, relate to what is to be used in the way of further resources as opposed to what would be achieved. A move to resource allocation decisions which are based on outputs rather than inputs is perhaps the fundamental change required in the health service. It has always been a matter of debate whether the services provided actually matched the need for services. Such discussions are fraught with difficulties, not the least of which is the process by which need ought to be determined. One quite widely accepted definition [42] is that 'need for medical care exists when an individual has an illness or disability for which there is an effective and acceptable treatment or cure. . . . A demand for medical care exists when an individual considers that he has a need and wishes to receive care. Utilisation occurs when an individual actually receives care.' Even ignoring for the moment the difficulties of agreeing those simple definitions two very important implications arise. The first is that need is unlikely to correspond with demand, demand does not ensure utilisation and there is likely to be demand and use without need. The second is that it is unlikely that there will be enough resources to meet all need or that there will ever be sufficient resources to do all that the sophisticated technology of a modern society could do in the way of providing health care. Choices will always, therefore, have to be made and it is important that the best possible means of making these choices are being used.

The argument is frequently made that such choices are virtually impossible or at the very least are totally unreasonable. Superficially it may seem that the services currently available must be needed or such care would not be provided. However it is only 100 years ago that medical practice was restricted to the situation in which a patient sought out a doctor and asked for advice. As a result what was asked for and, in effect, only what was asked for was provided. Today there are two major differences; first, experience has shown that it is not always in the patients' interests to wait for them to approach the doctor and, second, because of increasing knowledge and the resulting specialisation, it is less easy to relate what is apparently asked for to what is actually required. Despite the fact that our services have highly trained staff and the most up-to-date equipment it does not follow that what is required is always available or that what is available is always required. As diseases change so must services adapt; hence the need, which is not new, to be concerned whether current medical services have in fact adapted or whether they are getting too far out of step.

The question of recognising the reality of having to make choices in health leads back to the acceptance of priorities in medical care needs. Again this is not new. There has always been a public responsibility for health; even before infection was understood quarantine and isolation existed. Apart, however, from these obvious public problems medical care was haphazard and covered only those patients who by choice or opportunity happened to go to a doctor. Unfortunately the problem of infectious disease could not be solved by just a few people seeking medical advice because the basic need was not merely to treat people who were sick but also to change or, if that was not possible, to control the behaviour of people before they became ill. This still applies in chronic disease. Because of this it has been suggested that health care is far too important to leave to doctors; it is certainly the case that health care is also far too important to leave until you are ill. To some extent this has led to the problems of clinicians deriving priorities only on the experience of patient contacts. When the health service started there were so many deficiencies that vast additional resources had to be provided with the result that those services capable of using the money immediately grew faster. Each favoured service developed its own separate momentum and grew in terms of what it was technically capable of doing for the patients it saw rather than for what was actually needed by the people it never saw. Sir Keith Joseph when he was Secretary of State for Health and Social Services said 'This is a very fine country to be acutely ill or injured in but take my advice and do not become old or frail or mentally ill here' [33]. There is imbalance in the services; some have fallen behind or have not been developed and, given that resources in terms of money and people are not unlimited, how are the priorities to be rearranged? Choices have to be made between providing simple help for people who can not feed themselves or go to the toilet unaided and providing operations for people who need new hip joints. These choices make people uneasy yet a moment's thought will indicate that because resources are known to be limited such decisions are already being made – but they are not obvious and therefore not generally recognised.

It is not the purpose or responsibility of health economists to make such choices. These can only be made by society and the people working in the health service. The purpose of health economics is to indicate the problems of decision-making and detail the alternatives so that the issues involved and the choices made are clearly understood.

Choice remains the critical issue. The health service today is a conglomeration of activities – some new, some old, some big, some small; the objectives are to save lives, to reduce morbidity and to provide care and comfort. Some services do all three and some concentrate more on one than on others. Because of these permutations all the aims of the health service can not be met in full and choices have to be made both within these aims and between them. Unfortunately the relative or comparative size of these concessions between specialties and groups of patients may be uneven and it is difficult to resolve because some of the judgements are subjective and will remain so because the values and information upon which the judgements might be made are not available or can not be quantified. On the other hand the position is only uncertain rather than out of control. It is probably fair to suggest that the present disposition of resources is of the right order and it is the edge rather than the core that might be adjusted. Indeed small percentage changes, for example between the allocations to the acute and chronic services, would over the years make a significant difference in the resources available to these services. The shift should be gradual to allow the one group of services time to adjust to a slower rate of growth but equally it is required to allow the other services time to develop effective uses of the additional resources.

Even in life-threatening conditions resources are not pumped in indefinitely. There comes a point when it is obvious that resources are being taken away from another activity so that the benefit of lives saved in the one is less than the number of lives lost in the other – here, as in the case of cardiac resuscitation and anaesthesia, the trade-off can be seen and calculated [66]. Different trade-offs could be identified at different margins and at different levels first within life-threatening conditions and second between life-threatening conditions and those providing care and comfort. And here the direction of trade-off may not always be that which superficial consideration might suggest. Death under some circumstances may well carry less priority when set against years of living in suffering. It is, as already indicated, a matter of values.

What is essential to recognise is that trade-offs are and have to be made. Such choices may mean less care of a particular type than could be given and it is not a sufficient justification in demanding more resources to say that lives will be saved or better care given; it ought primarily to be shown that the policy being promoted results in greater benefit than could be obtained by using the resources elsewhere or in another way.

These are, of course, just a few examples of the difficult decisions which the health service has not so far faced up to; although attempts have been made to move resources into apparently deprived categories of care the stimulus to pursue this approach has been lessened by the fact that the total resources available each year have increased in real terms. The illusion has been created that choice could be avoided to a large extent by limiting the questions to which services should be expanded and by how much. It is against this background and within this framework that health economics must be applied.

From what has been stated previously it is clear that, initially, more professionally trained economists need to be attracted into the health field. Within the discipline of economics, health economics is an area which is growing in importance and in the number of economists who are being attracted by its activities. Expansion can be assisted in two main ways. First, departments of economics in universities and polytechnics need to be made more aware of the potential that exists for the application of economics to health and health care problems, thereby making graduands more knowledgeable. Second, the health service itself and the relevant departments of health need to provide greater opportunities for economists to enter the field. Both could be achieved in a number of ways and it is for debate how best it can be done.

There is an urgent need for the development of the discipline of health economics and this might be approached initially through specialist units, perhaps university-based but jointly funded by the central departments and the health service. Such specialist units would develop the formal approach of health economics and modify and develop economic thinking and techniques to the health scene. Such units might also perform a large part of the teaching role envisaged and at the same time serve as a training base for economists interested in a career in the health service. As with the introduction of any new professional group, if the health service and the relevant health ministries are serious about using health economics then the critical consideration is to provide the opportunities and an attractive career structure.

In addition, or perhaps still as a part of such specialist units, lectureships in health economics might be funded, such appointments being joint between departments of economics and community medicine. Such lectureships would provide the manpower for the teaching of health economics both in universities – in economics departments and faculties of medicine – and in the health service.

Health economics is still a relatively young branch of the discipline of economics. Consequently there is considerable scope for drawing on the corpus of knowledge in that discipline and reforming and developing it to make it more appropriate to the health care field. For example, much work remains to be done by economists on the issues of health output measurement and valuation. When the stage of self generation has been attained the health economics teams could then concentrate on the role of innovation and experiment.

But perhaps the most important step would be to ensure that a sufficient number of people at all levels and in all sections of the health service appreciate the significance of the basic principles of economics as they are applied to health care. Issues such as trade-offs, implied values, opportunity costs, social values, least cost solutions and marginal analysis are all vital to the determination of priorities. It is not enough for just a few people to understand such thinking; what is required is that many more people in and associated with the health service should think in terms of economics and be able to communicate with economists and that, in addition, some people should have sufficient experience actually to apply the related techniques. This does not mean that even at present there is no economic thinking in the health service but rather that the appreciation and opportunity are not as great as is necessary. Many people, of course, are aware of the issues; what has been missing has been the appropriate environment in which to develop these intuitive attitudes into an established or formal approach by the health service to the questions of decision-making and determining priorities. To this end there is a need to expand basic introductory courses in health economics for health authority members, local health councils and professional and administrative staff. In addition, opportunities will also be required for certain categories of health service staff to undertake more detailed study and to apply economic techniques to particular health service problems.

The best way of spreading knowledge and understanding depends on the ultimate goal. If that goal is seen as a general understanding by a proportion of the staff coupled with a more predominant role by management accountants so that policy evolves from a wider participation by the staff and the public then the concept of specialist units, providing training and techniques to achieve the necessary momentum, is perhaps the better approach.

If on the other hand the aim is ultimately to establish economists as members of planning teams determining, as well as informing on, policy then the most likely way of achieving it would be to concentrate on appointing health economists as officers of individual health boards and authorities. In this way the specialist skills of economists would be most readily available to the health service. However, such economists might suffer from being isolated from fellow economists. There is then much to be said for linking such appointees to more senior health economists located outside the specific authority, perhaps in a local academic establishment. Despite the small number of trained people available there is, in practice, no real conflict between setting up specialist units and spreading economics through the health service.

Yet another model involves economists in academic units providing consultancy services to the health service either on specific problems as they arise or on a continual basis contributing, say, two days a month of economic advice. The advantage of this is that it is more likely to be based on an identified and explicit demand for an economist's services. It is also less costly than appointing a full-time economist.

Whichever approach is adopted, the top priority remains one of education. Unless more economists are made aware of health service problems and more health service staff appreciate the need for economic efficiency and hence the value of economic analysis, then economics in health care will remain underutilised.

There is an unfortunate tendency, perhaps fostered by the present structure of the service, for people to interpret their roles somewhat narrowly and to look to others to provide what else is required. This problem is well illustrated in the matter of information; few people in the health service can function effectively without it yet despite this even fewer people define in advance their information needs and actively participate in its collection. It appears to be assumed that because an information service exists it absolves everyone else from responsibility and action. The fact is seldom acknowledged, although Körner has gone some way to overcome the problem [21], that those who operate the information services can not really be expected to anticipate all the requirements, supervise all the collection and undertake all the analysis and interpretation. There should be team exercises where all the participants understand and appreciate the contributions of everyone else. There is a danger that even the most basic appreciation of health economics remains a specialist function and one of the most appropriate means of avoiding this would be to introduce the application of economic principles into the day to day thinking of health service operations. It is perhaps more important that people really understand the philosophy of health economics rather than have obtained a passing familiarity with, or even experience of, isolated health economic techniques.

An avowed intention for the health service in the future is a greater participation by both the public and all health service employees in policy and management. The price of such participation will have to be a greater understanding of and commitment to the essential functions upon which policy-making and management should be based. This must include obtaining and interpreting information, absorbing and acknowledging the philosophy of choice and accepting and abiding by the inevitable constraints of planning procedures. Such ventures can only be built on experience and opportunity and the extent to which these already exist is therefore a key factor in assessing the likely success of more general participation in health service management.

Opportunities vary but the greatest scope to apply the techniques and approach of health economics is to be found at local level. It might appear that even greater scope would lie with the central departments but, apart from some small pre-empting of expenditure and a similarly small measure of specific coercion for a particular form of development, the opportunity for decision-making, in theory if not yet in practice, has been delegated. At region in England, and at area in Scotland, perhaps the most significant development would be an adoption of programme budgeting through which it would be possible to set both short and long term objectives. In turn the setting of quantified financial allocations would allow developments to be monitored and would maintain a consistency even when decisions are made at different times throughout the year. Then the implications of each decision could be set against the revenue objectives for the coming year. Priorities between individual services would first be set by the budgets allocated and thereafter competitive priorities would have to be ordered within each programme against the total sum available and the various demands being made.

On a much smaller scale the advantages of programme budgeting could also be obtained by specific service departments with knowledge of the resources available and a clearly defined individual or group with authority to commit them. Laboratories and certain of the discrete para-clinical services such as physiotherapy could adopt the approach and control excessive or unpredicted demand for particular items by increasing waiting times. The clinical services, although theoretically able to operate programme budgets, are in practice restricted in pursuing such developments because of the diverse control of individual resources and a lack of detailed financial data specific to their activities. None the less the extent of the resources committed in this way means that some way must be found of offering the same opportunities to the health care professionals to reallocate their clinical budgets or the full benefits of programme budgeting will never be obtained. Indeed, the operation of programme budgeting at one level of decision-making without a corresponding option at each of the succeeding levels would merely perpetuate the frustration and lack of commitment that already exists.

Programme committees and health care planning teams, as the only truly multi-professional groups reporting to the boards and authorities, are another medium through which various principles of economics can be applied. As their responsibility is to produce plans and options for implementation the importance to them of matters such as marginal analysis, least cost solutions, opportunity costs and cost–benefit analysis are obvious. Ideally the presentation of the options by these groups should be derived from the appropriate analysis and it is in such issues that the dilemma of whether to concentrate or disperse the economic skills likely to be available to the health service becomes manifest. Initially at least, those areas with access to economists will be at a distinct advantage. In time the presence on such groups of management accountants with the necessary skills would mark a departure not merely in practice but in outlook on the part of the health service. There has been a tendency to view the activities of the staff of the treasurer's department as being restricted to the legality or appropriateness of particular payments rather than the wisdom and value of the individual purchases. It is unrealistic to expect the different professions to acquire the skills and understanding of their various professional colleagues and the object of a management team will never be achieved unless each of the members is given the opportunity to make his appropriate contribution.

A case in point is the whole question of the opportunity costs of proposed developments and even of existing services. The only sensible approach is to define a series of options or alternative packages which may not all be viewed favourably by particular professional groups but which must at least be acknowledged as feasible. It is only after the possible alternatives have been listed that the advantages and disadvantages of their adoption should be argued by each professional group including accountants and administrators. It is astonishing how often a consideration of cost is still claimed to be inappropriate in such deliberations until after the decision has been made. The idea that costs should not be included in the early stages of the analyses is a legacy from the past. Although this may have been understandable when the National Health Service started, its continuation at the current level of expenditure will assuredly perpetuate any imbalance in the distribution of resources between services. The final decision should arise from a consideration of detailed analyses in which the interaction of the various options and the carry-over from previous decisions can be examined and appropriate trade-offs selected. Too often there is a tendency for individuals or professional groups to select immediately the best option from their point of view which very soon thereafter becomes the only option as far as they are concerned. Administrators themselves are inclined to follow a similar course and it is worth noting that too frequently health boards and authorities are still presented with single solutions to their problems; with experience this limitation is no longer acceptable to the members but it shows the extent to which attitudes and practices still have to change.

Within even this limited framework there are considerable possibilities for developing more systematic and overt procedures for reaching decisions. A concern on the part of boards and authorities mainly with the allocation of resources between services and departments and an equal but different responsibility on the part of the various services and departments to make certain the resources are used to the greatest effect within the values adopted could be attained by the use of the simple techniques described earlier in this book. More important, such approaches lead to the recognition and stating of objectives, albeit simple, the attainment and determination of which can be monitored and reargued. In this way the lessons of experience can be quantified and applied to decision-making problems in the future.

As suggested in the previous chapter, it is unrealistic to expect all staff to be involved in all decisions. It is more important that they should be knowledgeable about and involved in those issues concerned with the particular part of the service in which they work. The most serious disadvantage of the existing structure is its complexity. This is partly due to the genuine desire to afford staff a greater say in the running of the service and partly due to the structure that was required to ensure suitable career structures for all the people employed before integration. One might argue from this that administration of the health service is overmanned but it would be equally valid to assert that the staff are being asked to do the wrong things. More and more of the health service resource is required to run the system and correspondingly less is available for the provision of patient services. If it is unrealistic for staff to be overcommitted it is similarly inappropriate to expect health councillors to be aware of the pressures and problems of all the various services and better for a smaller number of members of the public to be closely associated with one particular, even if specialised, service. If this is accepted, the way to resolve most of the current difficulties would be to disaggregate the present structure into smaller discrete individual services – the so-called service programmes suggested in chapter 10. These could then be used not only as the basis for consultation, budgeting, management and planning but also as a direct and discrete channel of communication between the health board or authority, their staff and their patients.

Suggesting changes in the organisation of the service primarily to accommodate the application of health economics, creditable as such a venture might be, could not be justified; but the real issue is the need for more appropriately structured planning and decision-making processes with which, of course, health economics and its techniques are closely identified. In this respect at least the appointment of general managers may assist.

There are other implications in that people are so involved in attempting to sustain the present system that there is insufficient time actually to plan or manage the services. A great deal of ill-feeling has been directed at the administration of the health service and, as is the superficial tendency, has been concerned merely with the number of people employed for these purposes rather than the tasks which these people are being required to perform to keep the process of participation flowing. The fact that administration has been repeatedly criticised as wasteful is at least a partial explanation of why the Griffiths inquiry was set up [20].

Changes of the nature suggested would obviously facilitate a wider adoption of programme budgeting and would greatly increase the incentive to look at the possibility of change because any resources freed would be immediately available to the people making that change. Equally important would be a lessening of the feelings of frustration at not being granted additional support for development because no longer would the individuals involved be unable to act. It would be possible to re-examine the other priorities within the total programme of the specialty and decide whether or not the new development carried a higher priority than some of the existing activities. It might be argued that it is unfair that such decisions should have to be made by the health-care professional. This would be a misunderstanding; in reality the decision in terms of the budget allocations has already been made by parliament and by the board or authority and what is being given to the health-care professionals is the chance to determine that the best possible use is being made of the resources available. Management budgeting as proposed by Griffiths is a clear step in this direction.

By this means a new form of clinical freedom would also be established. The original need for this assurance has passed and, while resources are certainly limited, the fear that appropriate care might be unreasonably restricted primarily on the grounds of cost have not materialised. As a result the previous safeguard of not creating individual clinical budgets has now become a handicap and perhaps the major barrier to clinical freedom. For many reasons, therefore, alternatives should be examined. With a degree of flexibility, the benefits of delegating to the service programmes the authority to modify as necessary their activities within the general policy would mean a far greater likelihood that resources were used to the optimum. In addition those providing the services would feel involved, would see the results of their efforts, could set their own objectives and use the necessary techniques to assess their performance and achievement. In this way the essential environment would have been created to allow the application of the principles of health economics at the most practical level.

Nearly thirty years ago the Guillebaud Committee [44] (chaired by an economist) pointed out that 'in the absence of an objective and attainable standard of adequacy the aim must be to provide the best service possible within the limits of the available resources. . . . It is illusory to imagine that everything which is desirable for the improvement of the Health Service can be achieved at once.' Despite the fact that in real terms the health service is spending three times as much as when that report was written the statement still applies today as, of course, it will in another thirty years; need, demand and use are all relative to the current values of society at any particular time. These values inevitably change and the illusion that it will ever be different merely perpetuates dissatisfaction, frustration and suspicion. The realities of choice are not all that stark; a great deal of money, skill and goodwill exists and what is required is an atmosphere in which resources are used to the full rather than assumed to be inadequate from the start. The first step is for everyone to acknowledge the need for choice; thereafter the sequence of strategic and operational planning through day to day management will take on the much needed catalyst of realism.

A great deal of misunderstanding arises from the confusion and mixing of different forms and levels of decision-making in the health services. A separation is required of broad resource allocation decisions, which should be based on an assessment of current social values, from the detailed operational decisions which must be based on technical knowledge. At present in an attempt to obtain greater participation of both the public and staff these separate functions have become entangled.

On the other hand the importance of distinguishing between need, demand and use is well recognised. A great deal is known about which services are used but very little about what is achieved by the use of those resources. Despite the fact that this has been recognised for some time, surprisingly little progress has been made in developing suitable measures of outcome. Also, it is argued that so long as the allocation of resources is geared to inputs and not outputs the situation is unlikely to change. Both these problems are perpetuated by the health service structure and if further changes in the organisation of the service are contemplated then these issues should be borne in mind.

.Health care like health should involve everyone, at some point and in some way, but it is a mistake to try to involve everyone in all aspects of care because there is a limit to the range of issues that the majority of people can comprehend and in which they can attain competence.

Until the realities of choice and incentives to make choices are introduced into the health service the present superficial health planning and lack of willingness to get to grips with a reallocation of resources will persist. But in overcoming this inertia the principles and techniques of health economics can only help those who really want to change.

References

1. Sir W. Beveridge, *Social Insurance and Allied Services* (London: HMSO, 1942).
2. D. Boddy, 'Programme planning committees in the Greater Glasgow Health Board', *Health Bulletin*, **35**, 5 (1977) 271–81.
3. J. Bradshaw, 'A taxonomy of social need', in G. McLachlan (ed.), *Problems and Progress in Medical Care*, 7th series (Oxford University Press, 1972).
4. A. Burchell and B. K. Gilbert, *Appraisal of Development Options in the National Health Service* (London: DHSS, 1982).
5. Central Statistical Office, *Social Trends*, no. 9 (London: HMSO, 1979).
6. A. L. Cochrane, *Effectiveness and Efficiency: Random Reflections on Health Services* (London: Nuffield Provincial Hospitals Trust, 1972).
7. M. H. Cooper, *Rationing Health Care* (London: Croom Helm, 1975).
8. W. M. M. Craigmile, I. D. Fordyce and G. H. Mooney, 'Domiciliary care of the elderly', *Nursing Times*, **74**, 4 (1978) 13–15.
9. A. J. Culyer, R. J. Lavers and A. Williams, 'Social indicators: health', *Social Trends*, no. 2 (London: HMSO, 1971).
10. A. J. Culyer and A. K. Maynard, 'Cost effectiveness of duodenal ulcer treatment', *Social Science and Medicine*, **15c** (1981) 3–11.
11. R. F. F. Dawson, *Current Costs of Road Accidents in Great Britain* (Crowthorne: Road Research Laboratory, 1971).
12. Department of Employment, *Family Expenditure Survey 1975* (London: HMSO, 1976).
13. Department of Health and Social Security, *Management Arrangements for the Reorganised Health Service* (London: HMSO, 1972).
14. Department of Health and Social Security, *NHS Planning. The Use of Staffing Norms and Indicators for Manpower Planning*, DHSS Circular to Regional Administrators, London, 1978.
15. Department of Health and Social Security, *Priorities for Health and Personal Social Services in England* (London: HMSO, 1976).
16. Department of Health and Social Security, *Sharing Resources for Health in England*. Report of the Resource Allocation Working Party (London: HMSO, 1976).
17. Department of Health and Social Security, *The Way Forward.*

Priorities in the Health and Social Services (London: HMSO, 1977).

18. Department of Health and Social Security, *Regional Chairman's Enquiry into the Working of the DHSS* (London: DHSS, 1976).
19. Department of Health and Social Security, *Patients First* (London: HMSO, 1979).
20. Department of Health and Social Security, *NHS Management Inquiry* (The Griffiths Report) (London: DHSS, 1983).
21. Department of Health and Social Security, *Health Services Information* (London: HMSO, 1982).
22. Department of Health and Social Services, *You and Your Baby*. Report of the Advisory Committee on Infant Mortality and Handicap in Northern Ireland (The Baird Report) (Belfast: HMSO, 1980).
23. Department of Health for Scotland, *Hospital Plan for Scotland* (Edinburgh: HMSO, 1962).
24. M. F. Drummond, *Principles of Economic Appraisal in Health Care* (Oxford: Oxford Medical Publications, 1980).
25. M. F. Drummond, *Studies in Economic Appraisal in Health Care* (Oxford: Oxford Medical Publications, 1981).
26. M. F. Drummond and G. H. Mooney, 'Economic appraisal in health care', *Hospital and Health Services Review* (1981) 277–82; 308–13.
27. S. Fanshel, 'The welfare of the elderly: a systems analysis viewpoint', *Policy Sciences*, 6 (1975), 343–57.
28. M. S. Feldstein, *Economic Analysis for Health Service Efficiency* (Amsterdam: North-Holland, 1967).
29. M. Foot, *Aneurin Bevan* (London: Macgibbon & Kee, 1962).
30. D. Gould, 'A groundling's notebook', *New Scientist*, 51 (1971) 217.
31. Grampian Health Board, *Reports of Study Group on Health Care Services* (unpublished, 1975).
32. A. M. Gray and R. Steele, *Programme Budgeting in Maternity Care*. HERU Discussion Paper (University of Aberdeen, 1979).
33. D. H. Greegor, 'Detection of silent colon cancer in routine examination', *CA*, 19 (1969), 330–7.
34. J. B. Henderson, A. McGuire and D. Parkin, *Acute hospital beds in Fife*, HERU series of option appraisal papers, nos 3 and 5 (University of Aberdeen, 1984).
35. J. B. Henderson, C. Beattie, E. Hale and T. Wright, 'The evaluation of new services: possibilities for preventing congenital toxoplasmosis', *International Journal of Epidemiology*, 13, 1 (1984) 65–72.
36. J. Jewkes and S. Jewkes, *The Genesis of the British National Health Service* (Oxford: Basil Blackwell, 1961).
37. M. W. Jones-Lee, *The Value of Life: An Economic Analysis* (London: Martin Robertson, 1976).
38. Sir K. Joseph, reported in *Western Morning News*, 30 June 1973.
39. H. E. Klarman, J. O's. Francis and G. D. Rosenthal, 'Cost–effectiveness analysis applied to the treatment of chronic renal failure', *Medical Care*, 6 (1968) 48–54.
40. M. Knapp, *The Economics of Social Care* (London: Macmillan, 1984).

41. K. Lee and A. Mills, *Policy-Making and Planning in the Health Sector* (London: Croom Helm, 1982).
42. G. K. Matthew, 'Measuring need and evaluating services', in G. McLachlan (ed.), *Portfolio for Health* (Oxford: Oxford University Press, 1971).
43. Ministry of Health, *A Hospital Plan for England and Wales* (London: HMSO, 1962).
44. Ministry of Health, *Report on Enquiry into the Cost of the NHS*, Cmnd. 9663 (London: HMSO, 1956).
45. E. J. Mishan, *Cost–Benefit Analysis* (London: George Allen & Unwin, 1971).
46. G. H. Mooney, 'Economic approaches to alternative patterns of health care', *Journal of Epidemiology and Community Health*, **33** (1979) 48–58.
47. G. H. Mooney, 'Planning for balance of care of the elderly', *Scottish Journal of Political Economy*, **25**, 2 (1978) 149–64.
48. G. H. Mooney, *The Valuation of Human Life* (London and Basingstoke: Macmillan, 1977).
49. G. H. Mooney, 'Screening for breast cancer, a case study in cost–effectiveness analysis', *Social Science and Medicine*, **16** (1982) 1277–83.
50. D. Neuhauser and A. M. Lewicki, 'What do we gain from the sixth stool guaiac?', *The New England Journal of Medicine*, **293** (1975) 226–8.
51. Office of Health Economics, *Understanding the NHS in the 1980's* (London: Office of Health Economics, 1984).
52. J. D. Pole, 'Programme, priorities and budgets', *British Journal of Preventive and Social Medicine*, **28**, 3 (1974) 191–5.
53. Report of the Committee on Nursing (the 'Briggs' Report), Cmnd. 5115 (London: HMSO, 1972).
54. Royal Commission on the NHS, Report, Cmnd 7615 (London: HMSO, 1979).
55. P. A. Samuelson, *Economics* (Tokyo: McGraw-Hill, 1976).
56. Scottish Home and Health Department, *Nurses in an Integrated Health Service* (Edinburgh: HMSO, 1972).
57. Scottish Home and Health Department, *Scottish Health Authorities Revenue Equalisation* (Edinburgh: HMSO, 1977).
58. Scottish Home and Health Department, *The Organisation of a Medical Advisory Structure* (Edinburgh: HMSO, 1973).
59. Scottish Home and Health Department, *The Health Services in Scotland. The Way Ahead* (Edinburgh: HMSO, 1976).
60. Scottish Home and Health Department, *Report of the Capital Steering Group* (Edinburgh: SHHD, 1984).
61. Scottish Home and Health Department, *Report of Ward Data Sub-Group* (Edinburgh: SHHD, 1984).
62. Scottish Home and Health Department, *Scottish Health Authorities Priorities for the Eighties* (Edinburgh: HMSO, 1980).

63. Scottish Home and Health Department, *Services for the Elderly with Mental Disability in Scotland* (The Timbury Report) (Edinburgh: HMSO, 1979).
64. P. R. Simpson, J. Chamberlain and H. S. E. Gravelle, 'Choice of screening test', *Journal of Epidemiology and Community Health*, **32** (1978) 166–70.
65. R. Sugden and A. Williams, *The Principles of Practical Cost Benefit Analysis* (Oxford: Oxford University Press, 1978).
66. T. H. Taylor, A. M. C. Jennings *et al.*, 'A study of anaesthetic emergency work, Paper V', *British Journal of Anaesthetics*, **41** (1969) 362–70.
67. R. Wager, *Care of the Elderly* (London: IMTA, 1972).
68. Welsh Office, *Report of the Steering Committee on Resource Allocation in Wales* (Cardiff: HMSO, 1978).
69. I. Wickings (ed.), *Effective Unit Management* (London: King's Fund, 1983).
70. I. Wickings, J. M. Coles, R. Flux and L. Howard, Review of Clinical Budgeting and Costing Experiments, *British Medical Journal*, 1983, **i**, 575–7.
71. A. Williams, 'The cost benefit approach', *British Medical Bulletin*, **30**, 3 (1974) 252–6.
72. A. Williams, 'Need an economic exegesis', in A. J. Culyer and K. G. Wright (eds), *Economic Aspects of Health Services* (London: Martin Robertson, 1978).
73. A. Williams and R. Anderson, *Efficiency in the Social Services* (Oxford: Basil Blackwell, and London: Martin Robertson, 1975).
74. World Health Organization, Official Records, No. 2, June, 1948.
75. K. G. Wright, 'Economics and planning the care of the elderly', in K. Lee (ed.), *Economics and Health Planning* (London: Croom Helm, 1978).
76. K. G. Wright, J. A. Cairns and M. C. Snell, *Report of a Research Project on Alternative Patterns of Care for the Elderly* (York: Institute of Social and Economic Research, 1979).

Select Bibliography

Costing, cost–effectiveness and cost–benefit studies in health care

M. J. Buxton and R. R. West, 'Cost–benefit analysis of long-term haemodialysis for chronic renal failure', *British Medical Journal*, **2** (1975) 376–9.

D. R. Cohen *et al.*, 'A cost-benefit study of milk borne salmonellosis', *Journal of Hygiene*, **91** (1983).

A. J. Culyer and A. K. Maynard, 'Cost–effectiveness of duodenal ulcer treatment', *Social Science and Medicine*, **15c** (1981) 3–11.

M. F. Drummond, *Studies in Economic Appraisal in Health Care* (Oxford: Oxford Medical Publications, 1981).

J. B. Henderson, 'Measuring the benefits of screening for open neural tube defects', *Journal of Epidemiology and Community Health*, **36**, 3 (1982) 214–9.

K. V. Lowson, M. F. Drummond and J. M. Bishop, 'Costing new services: long-term domiciliary oxygen therapy', *Lancet*, **1** (1977) 844–7.

A. Ludbrook, 'A cost–effectiveness analysis of the treatment of chronic renal failure', *Applied Economics*, **13** (1981) 337–50.

D. Neuhauser and A. M. Lewicki, 'What do we gain from the sixth stool guaiac?', *New England Journal of Medicine*, **293** (1975) 226–8.

E. M. Russell, *Patient Costing Study*, Scottish Health Services Studies, No. 31 (Scottish Home and Health Department, 1974).

P. R. Simpson, J. Chamberlain and H. S. E. Gravelle, 'Choice of screening tests', *Journal of Epidemiology and Community Health*, **32** (1978) 166–70.

Index